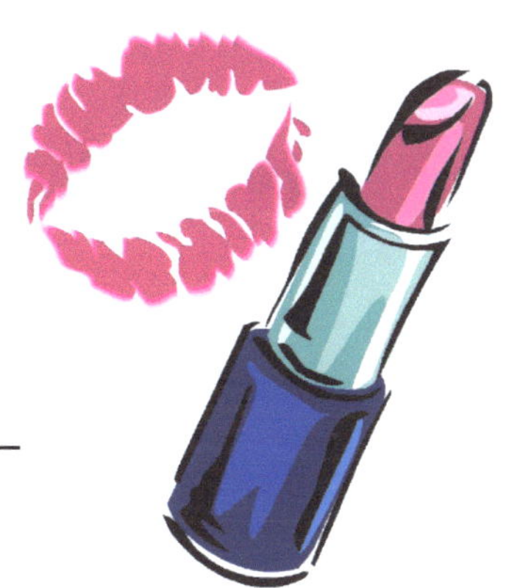



# World Famous Quotes

Gift Card

Date:

To:

From:

Message:

Art, Literature, Graphic Design, Poetry, Sharon Esther Lampert

# WORLD FAMOUS QUOTES SHARON ESTHER LAMPERT



**KADIMAH PRESS**
**GIFTS OF GENIUS**

Books may be purchased for education, business, or sales promotional use.
ISBN Hardcover:  9798348550875
ISBN Paperback:  9798348550882
ISBN e-book: 979-8-3485-5089-9
Library of Congress Control Number: 2025903445

**FAN MAIL:**
SharonEstherLampert.com
FANS@SharonEstherLampert.com

Cover and Interior Book Design: Creative Genius Sharon Esther Lampert
Editor: Dave Segal

Palm Beach Book Publisher, Phone: 917-767-5843
Sharon@PalmBeachBookPublisher.com
To Order Book:
Ingram, 1 Ingram Blvd. La Vergne, TN 37086-3629
Phone: 615-793-5000
Fax orders: 615-287-6990

First Edition

Manufactured in the United States of America

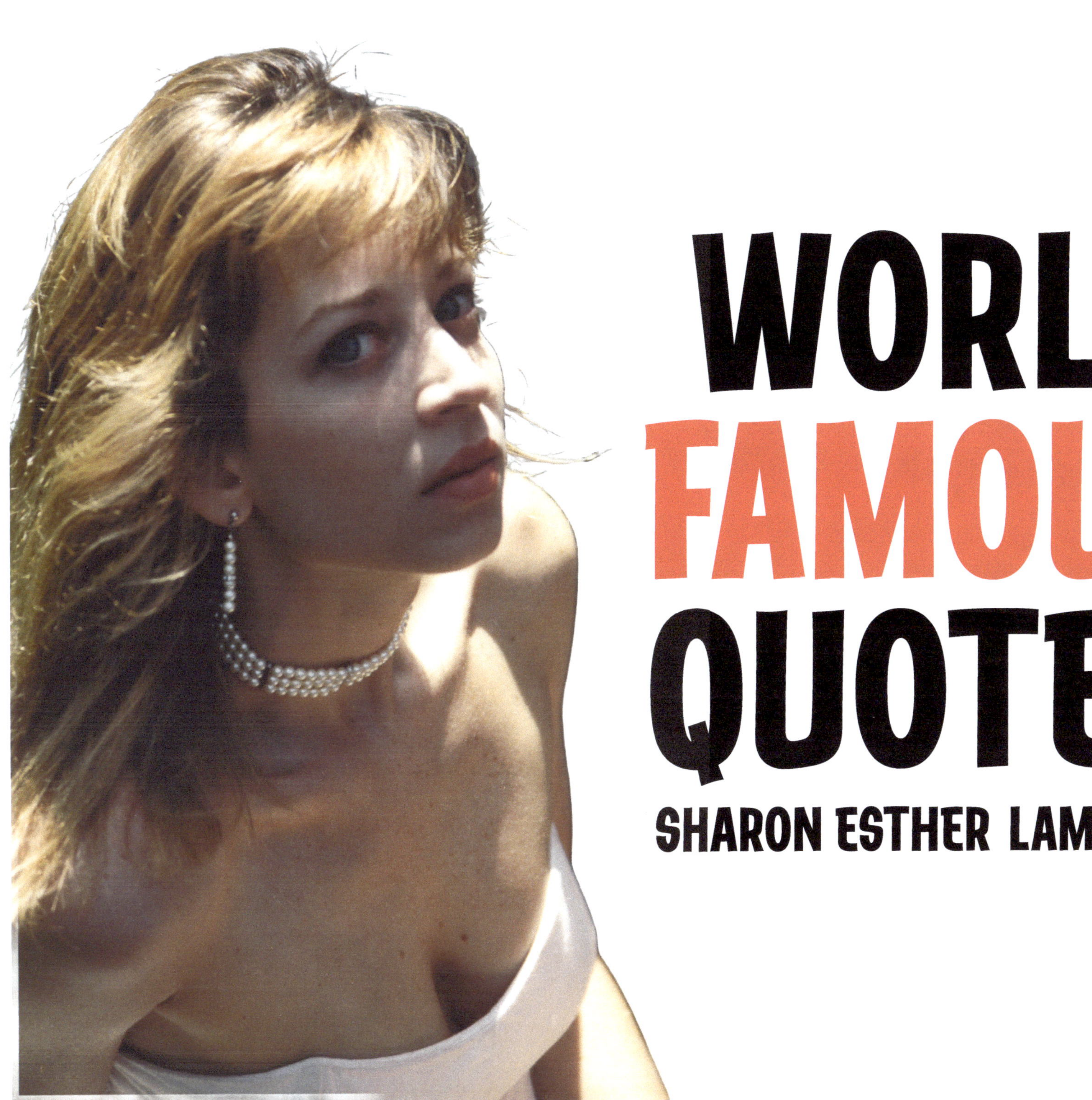

# WORLD FAMOUS QUOTES

## SHARON ESTHER LAMPERT

# Every Thought In Your Head Was Put There By a Writer!

*Sharon Esther Lampert*

# DEDICATION

## MOMMY

**LOVE** OF MY LIFETIME

WHO KNEW WHO I WAS FROM THE **INSIDE OUT**

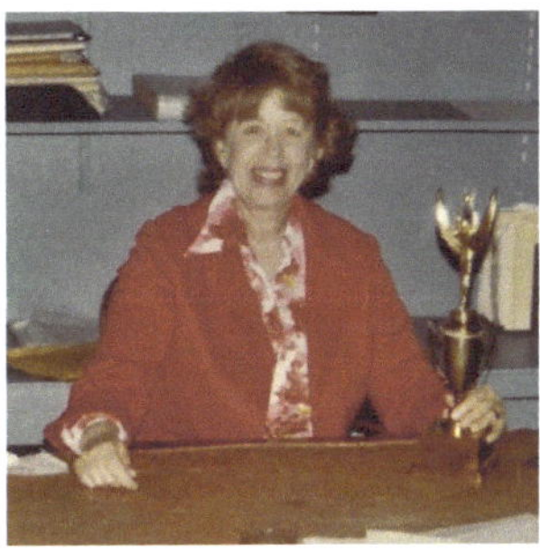

Age 9
THE QUEEN HAS ARRIVED!
My daughter is a poet,
philosopher, and teacher.
She is the Princess & Pea!
BEAUTY & BRAINS!
LOVE & XOXO
MOMMY

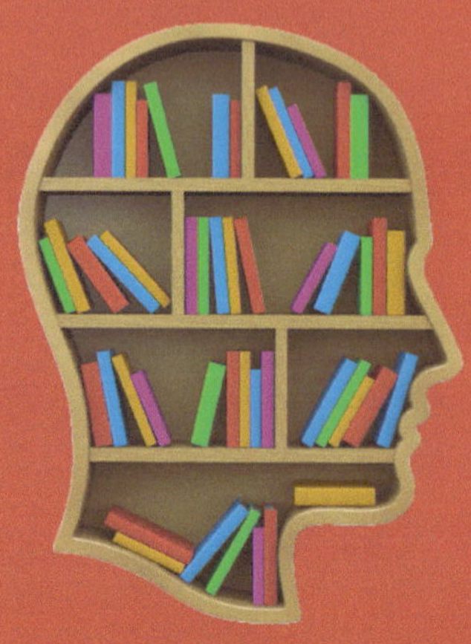

# What Do Books Do?
## BOOKS ARE POWERFUL

Books Educate!
Books Enlighten!
Books Empower!
Books Emancipate!
Books Entertain!
Books Spring Eternal!
Books Drive Exploration!
Books Spark Evolution!
Books Ignite Revolution!

Sharon Esther Lampert

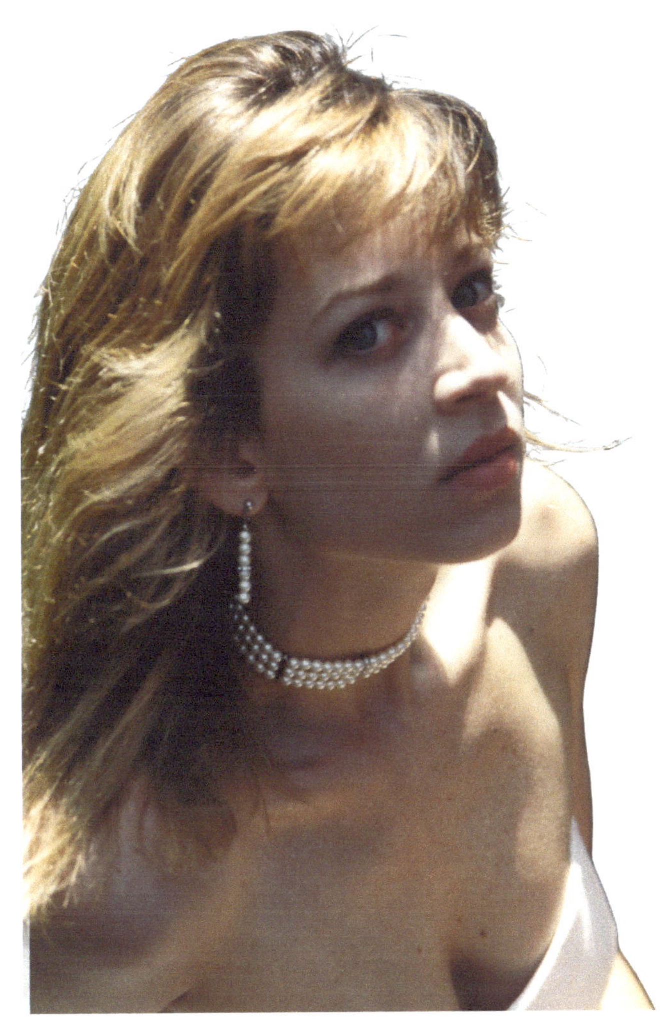

# WORLD FAMOUS QUOTES

## SHARON ESTHER LAMPERT

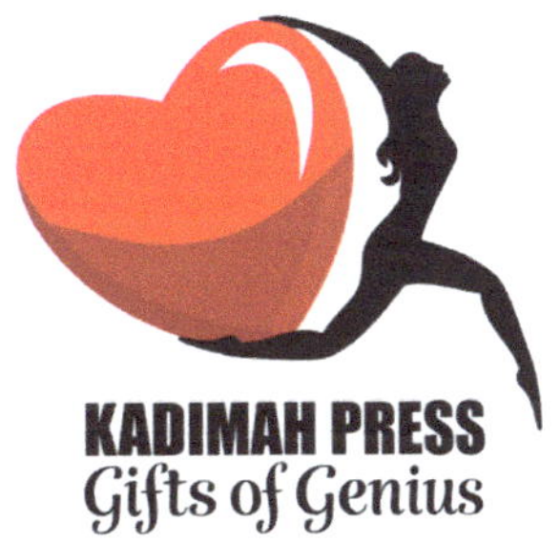

# What Is Art?

Art is the expression of the
soul of a human being.
When art moves you,
one soul has reached out
to touch another.

**SHARON ESTHER LAMPERT**
**PRODIGY, PROPHET, PHILOSOPHER, POET**
**PEACEMAKER, PHOTON SUPERHERO, PINUP**

SEE THE WORLD
THROUGH THE EYES
OF A CREATIVE GENIUS

# Table of Contents

# BE ART

ART IS SMART

ART IS FROM THE HEART

MAKE ART NOT WAR

YOU ARE BORN FOR GREATNESS

YOU ARE A MASTERPIECE

**Sharon Esther Lampert**

# Table of Contents

# LITERATURE IS POWERFUL BEYOND WORDS FOR IT CREATES WORLDS

Sharon Esther Lampert

# Table of Contents

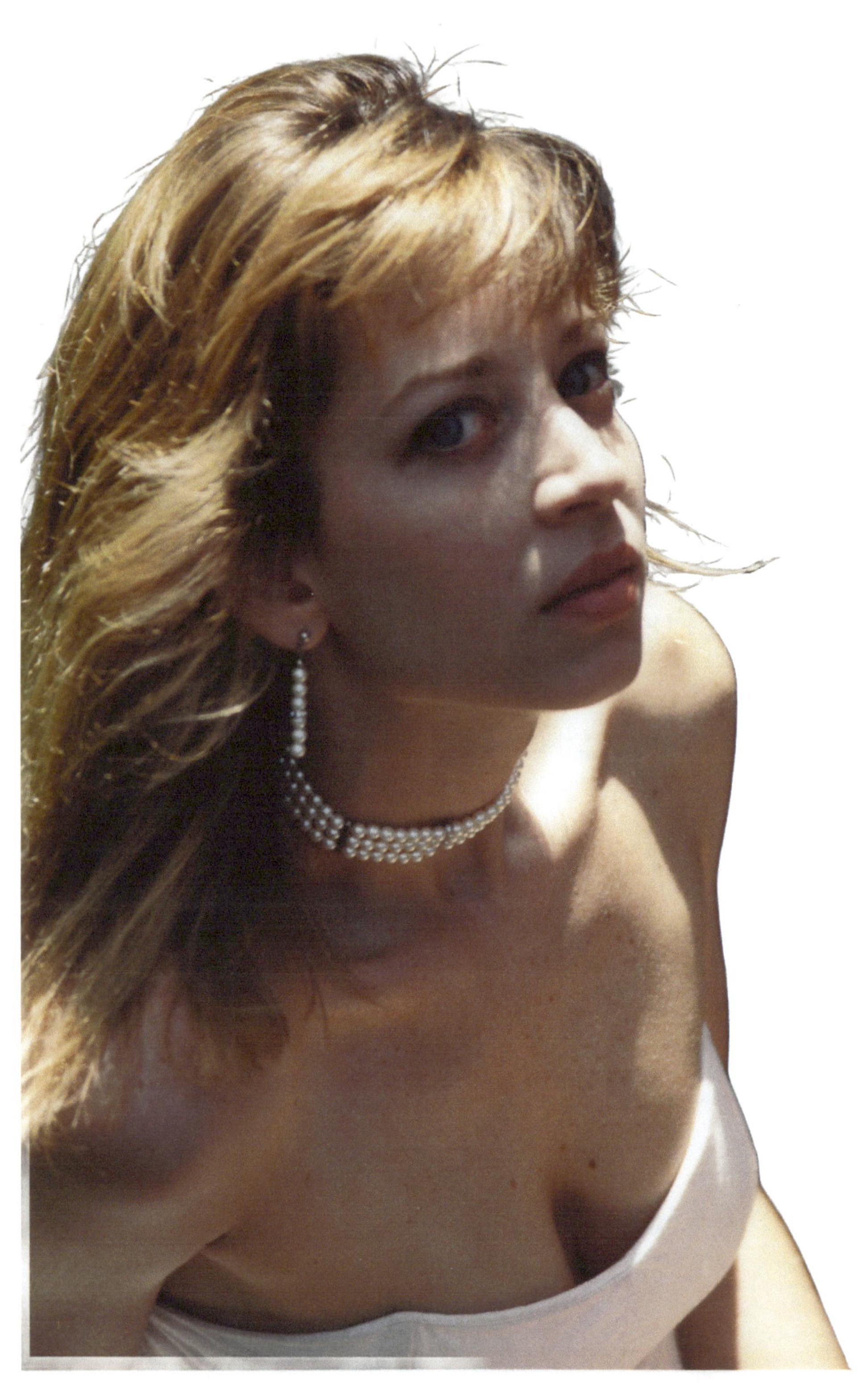

# FIGHT TO LIVE
# LIVE TO FIGHT
# BORN TO DIE

**Sharon Esther Lampert**

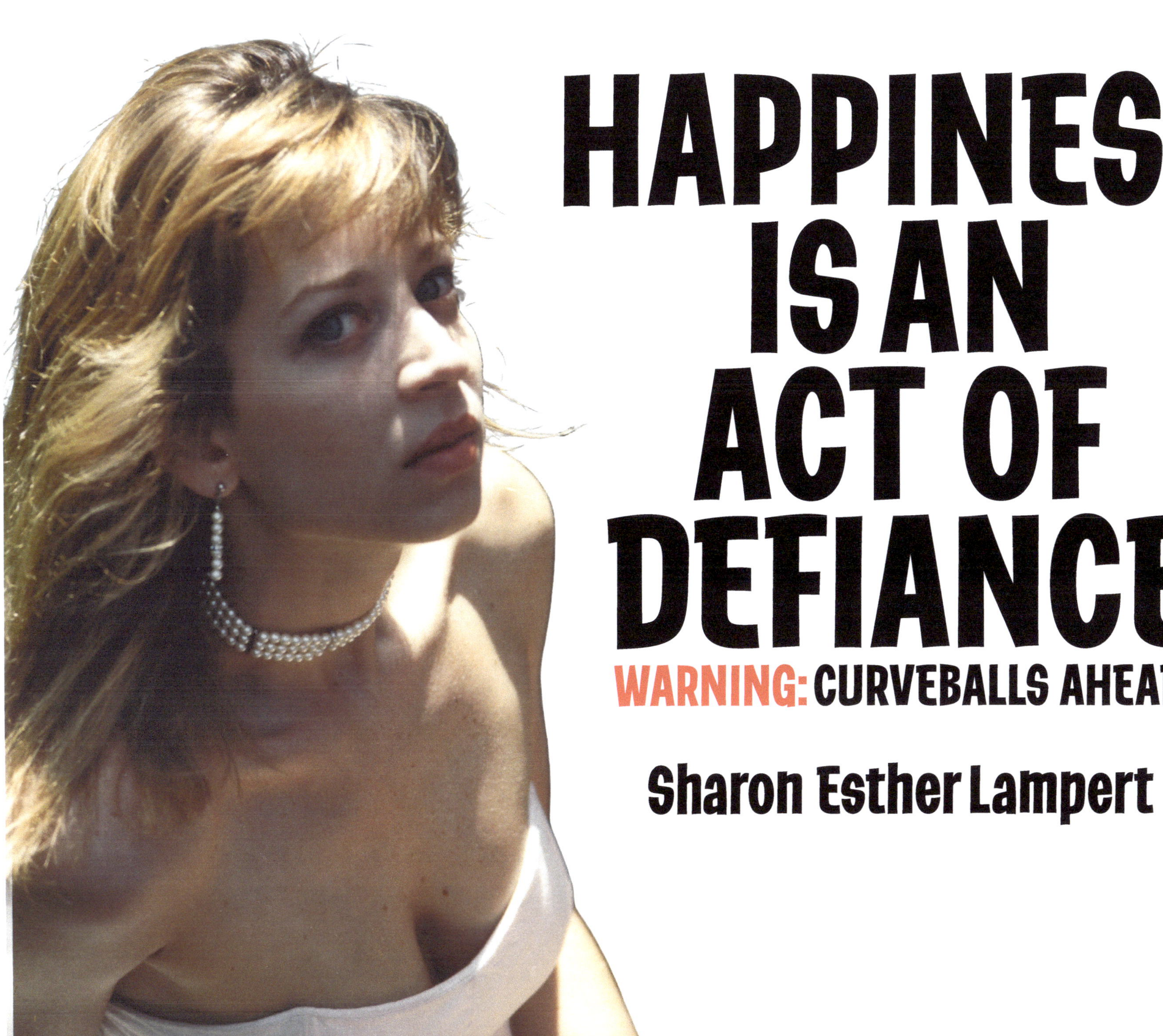

HAPPINESS IS AN ACT OF DEFIANCE
WARNING: CURVEBALLS AHEAD
Sharon Esther Lampert

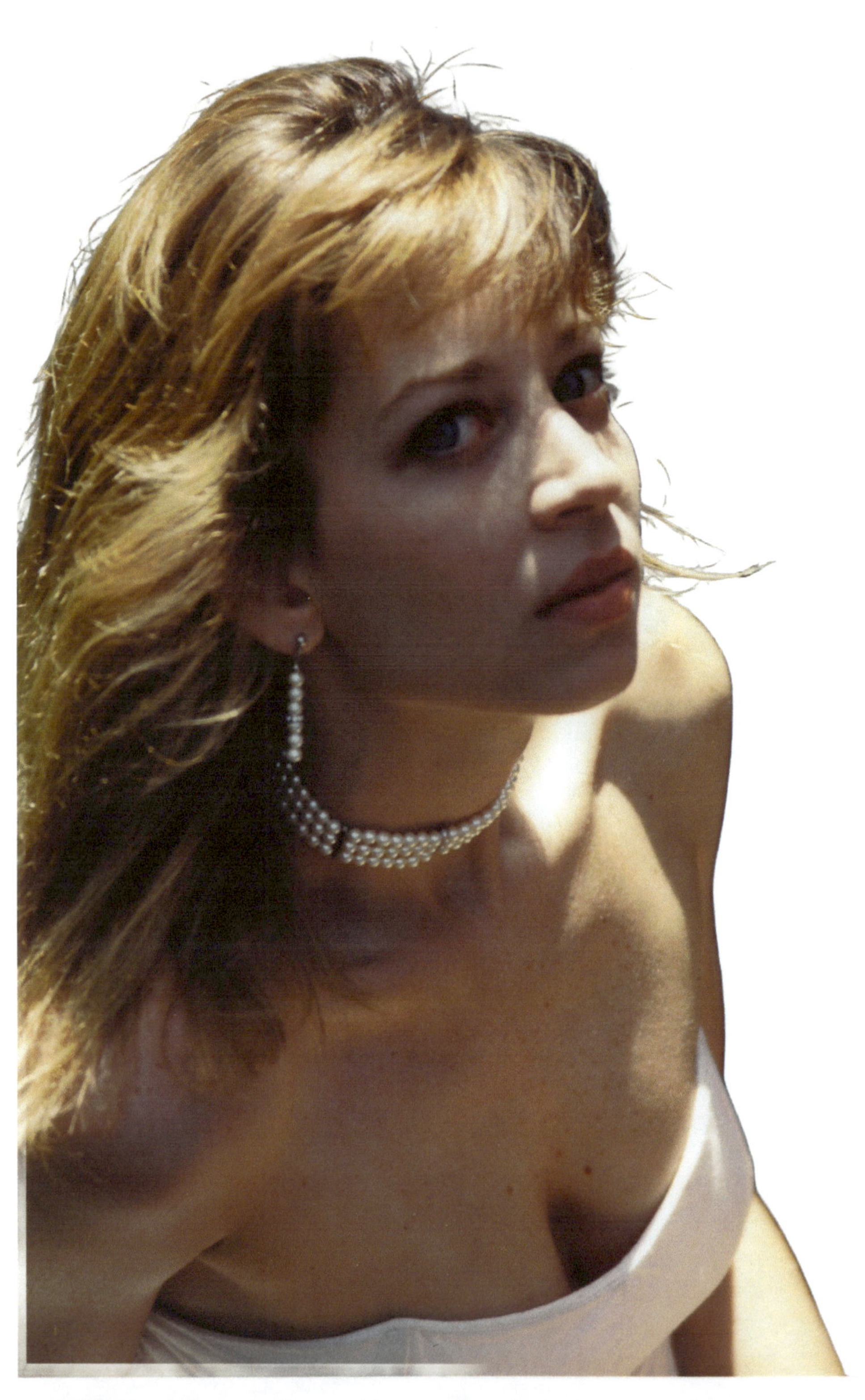

# FOOD
## Is For the BODY
# EDUCATION
## Is For the MIND
# POETRY
## Is For the SOUL

**Sharon Esther Lampert**

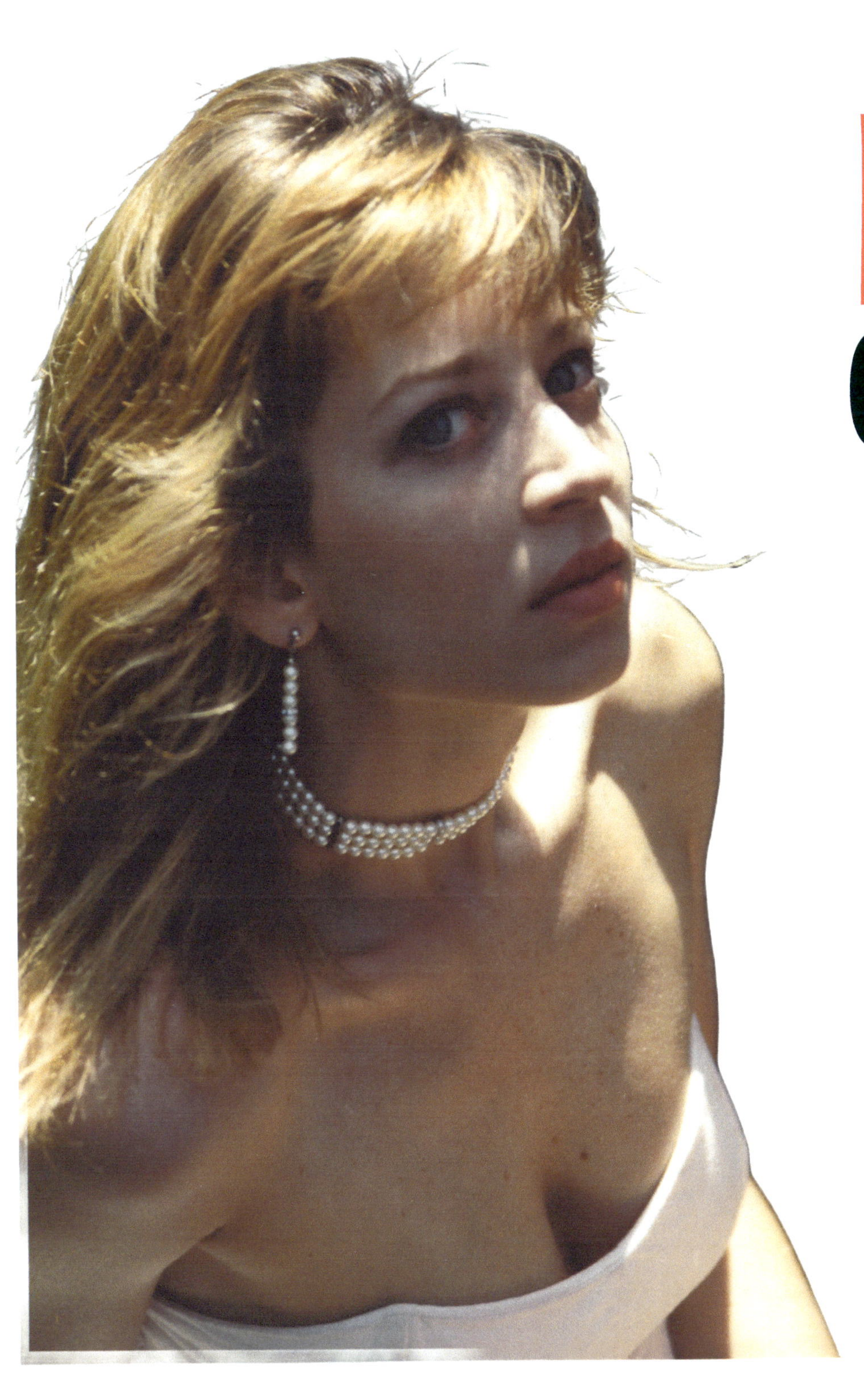
BE HARD
ON A WOMAN
ONLY WHEN
MAKING
LOVE
TO HER
Sharon Esther Lampert

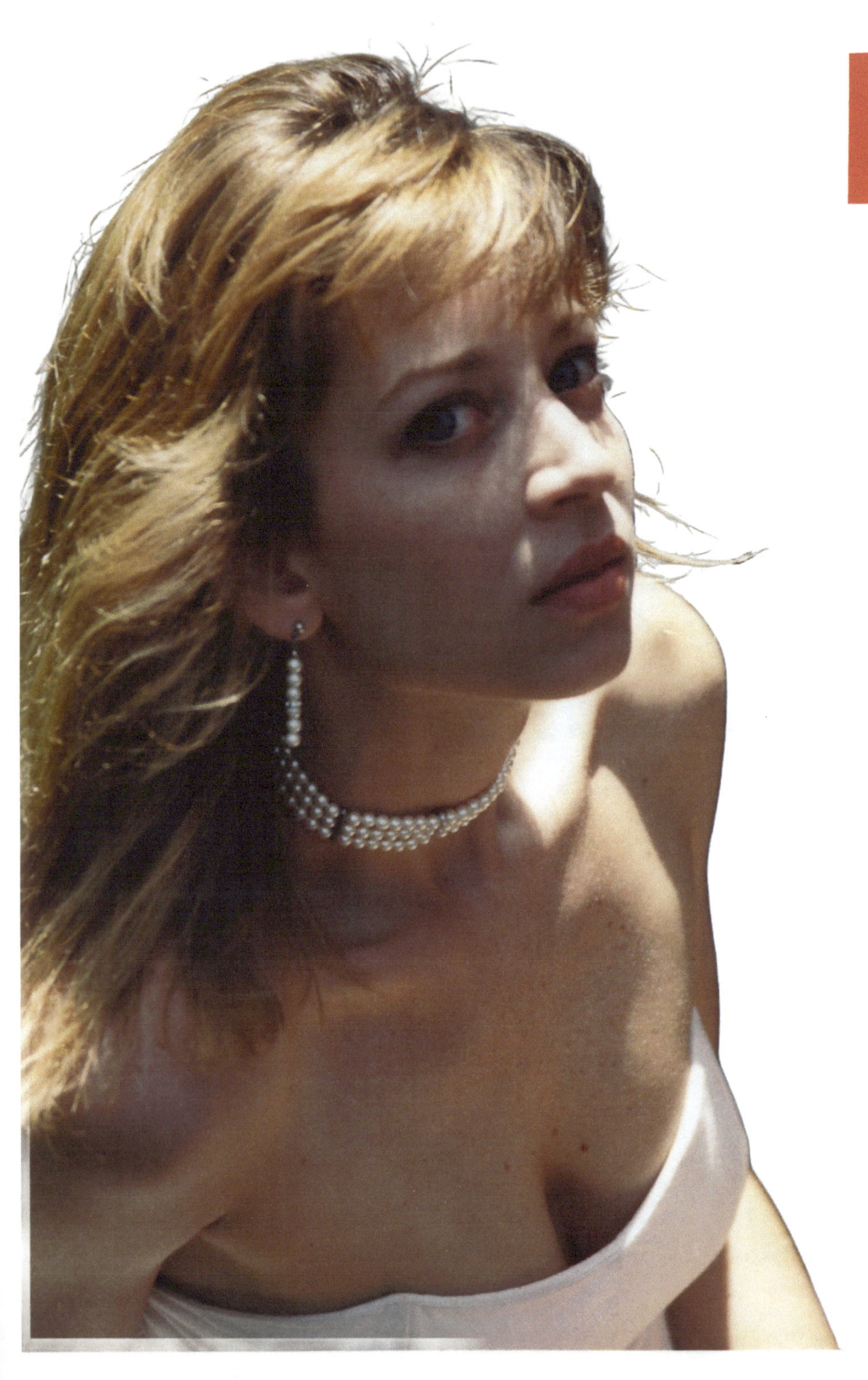

LOVE HURTS
AIDS KILLS
CONDOMS
RULE
LONG LIVE
SAFE SEX
Sharon Esther Lampert

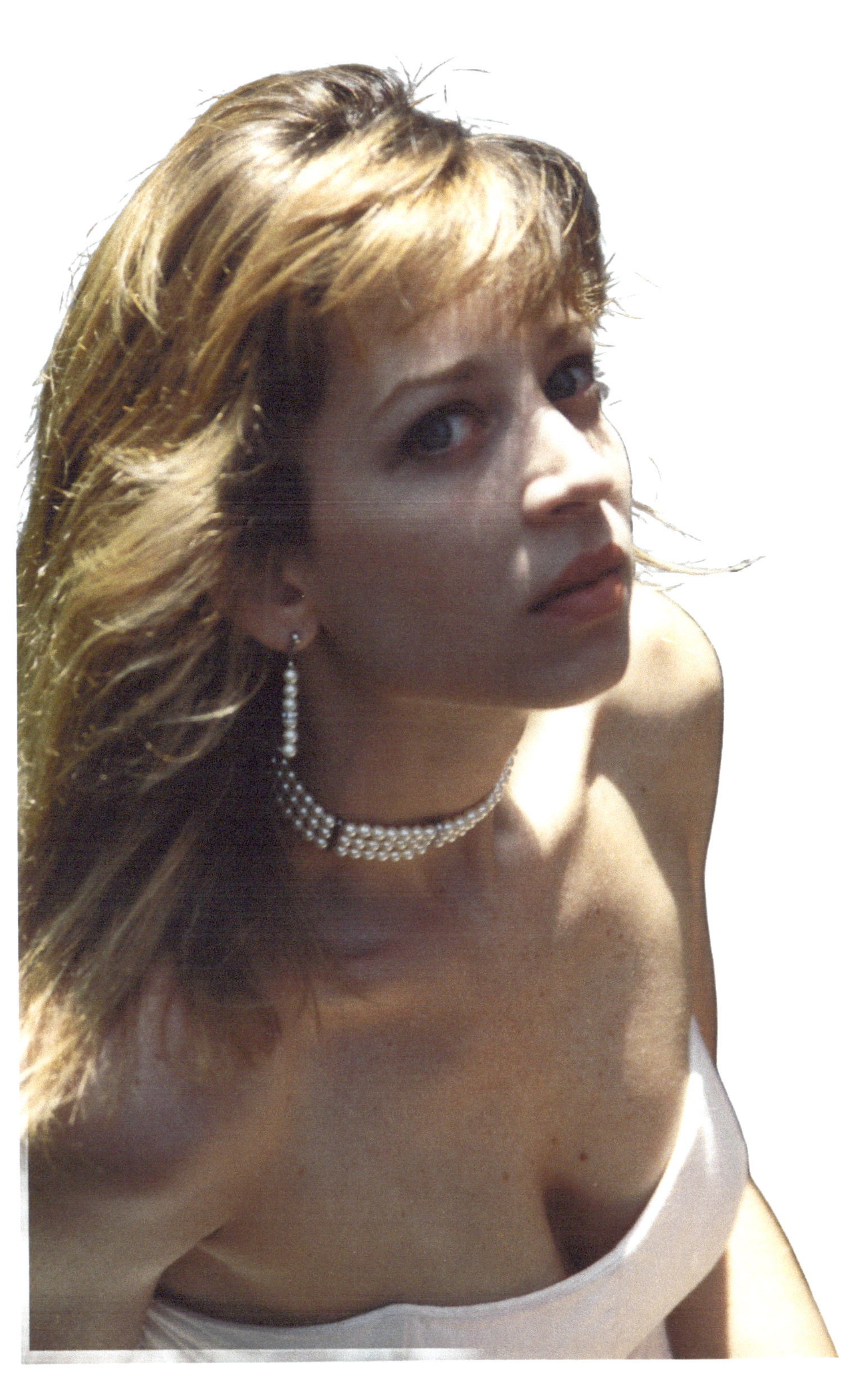

# THERE IS ONLY ONE **TRUTH** NO ONE HAS THE TRUTH

**Sharon Esther Lampert**

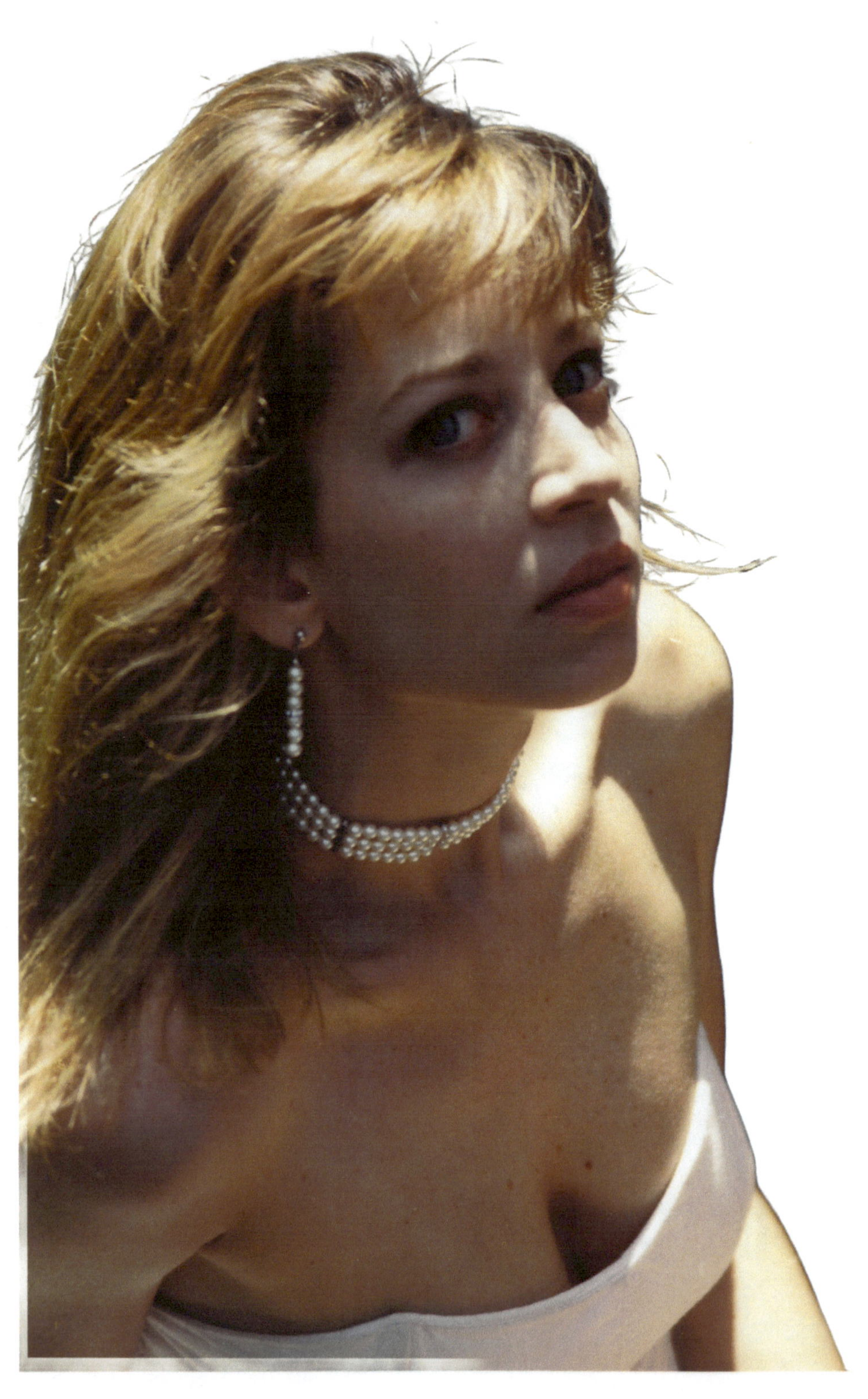

MY Life
Is an
OPEN Book
to
KNOW Me
Is to
READ Me

Sharon Esther Lampert

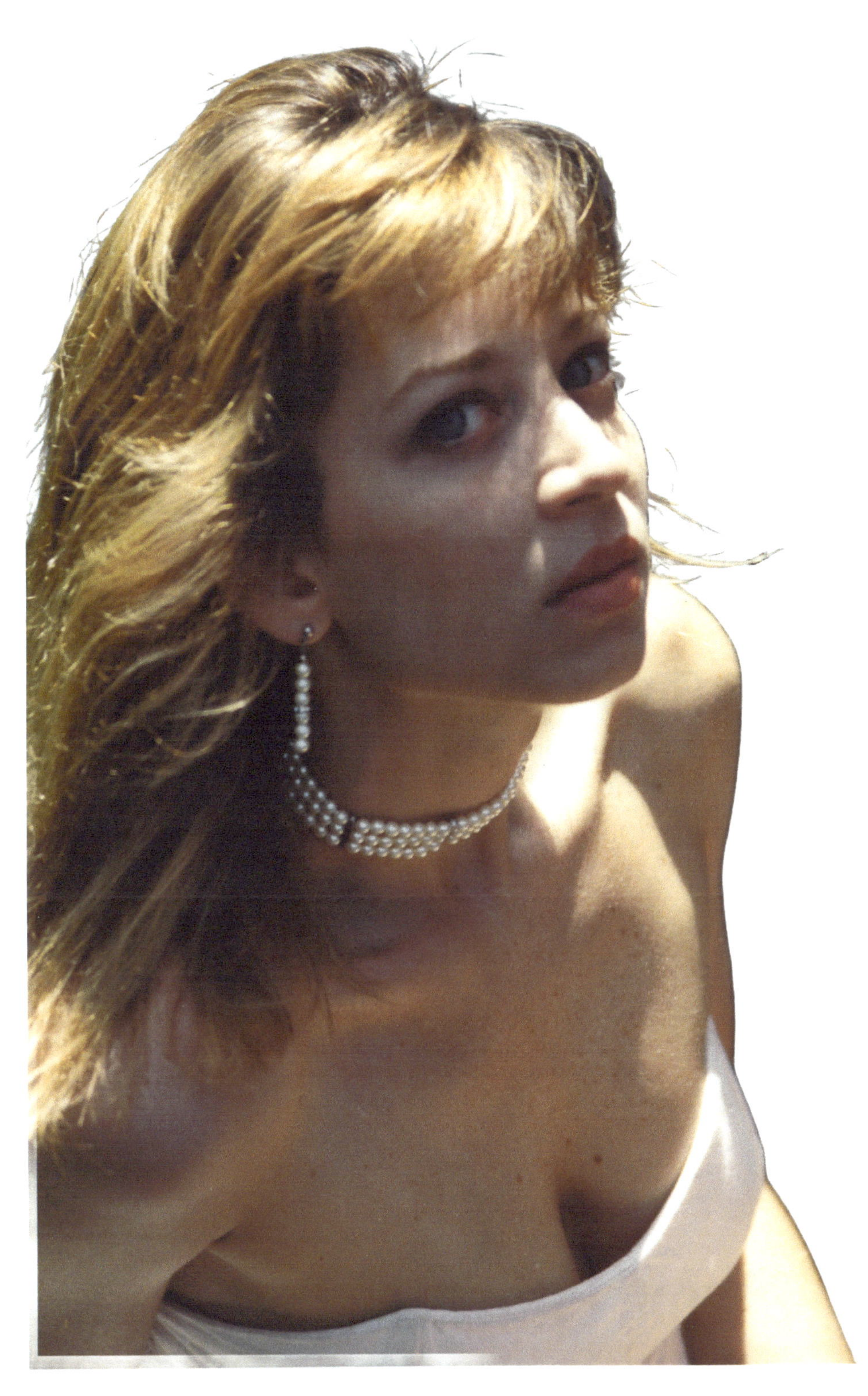

# The SOLE Intention of My POETRY Is to Add LIGHT to Your SOUL

**Sharon Esther Lampert**

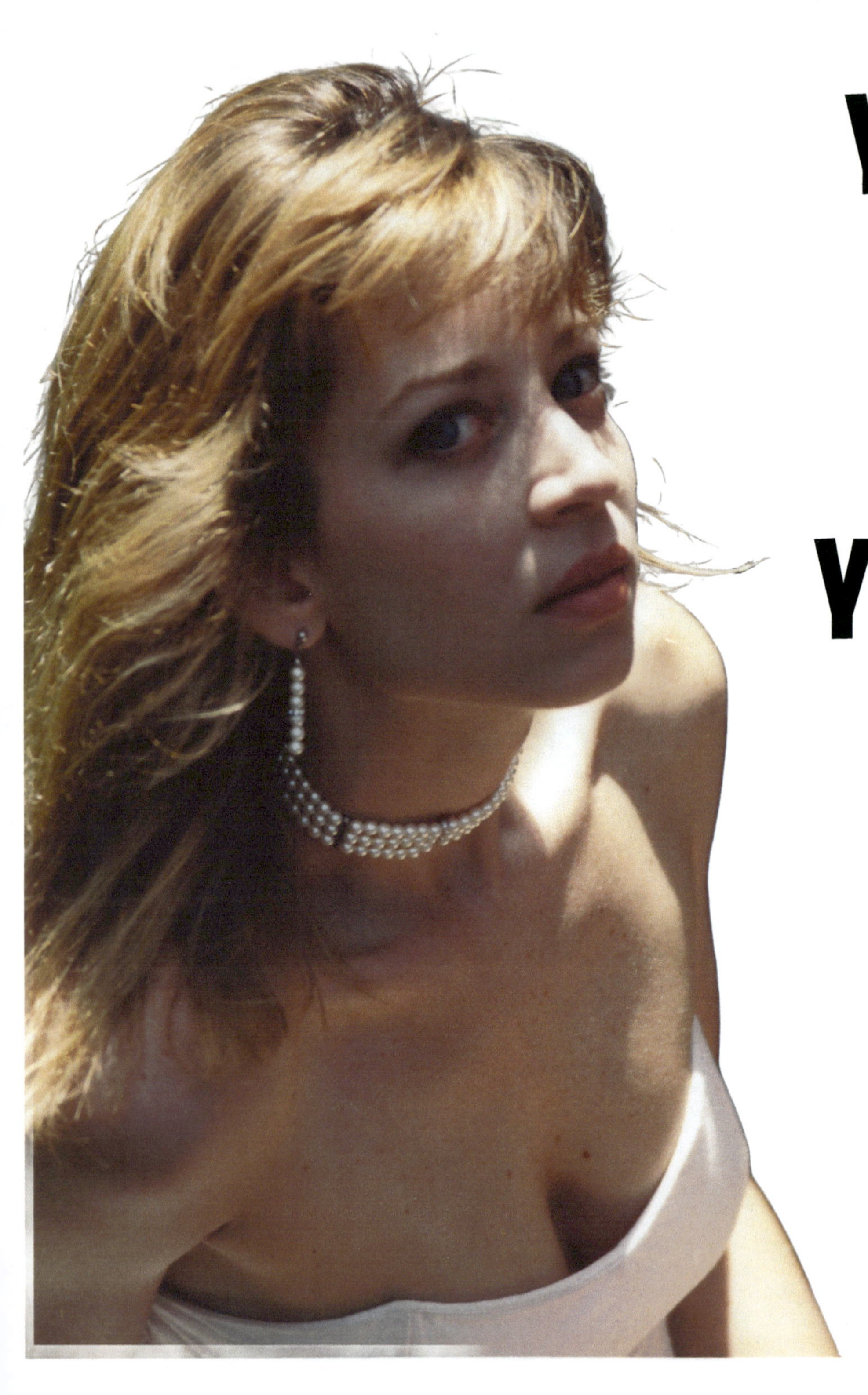
YOU DON'T FIND
LOVE
YOU CREATE LOVE
PRACTICE
RESPECT
KINDNESS
EMPATHY
Sharon Esther Lampert

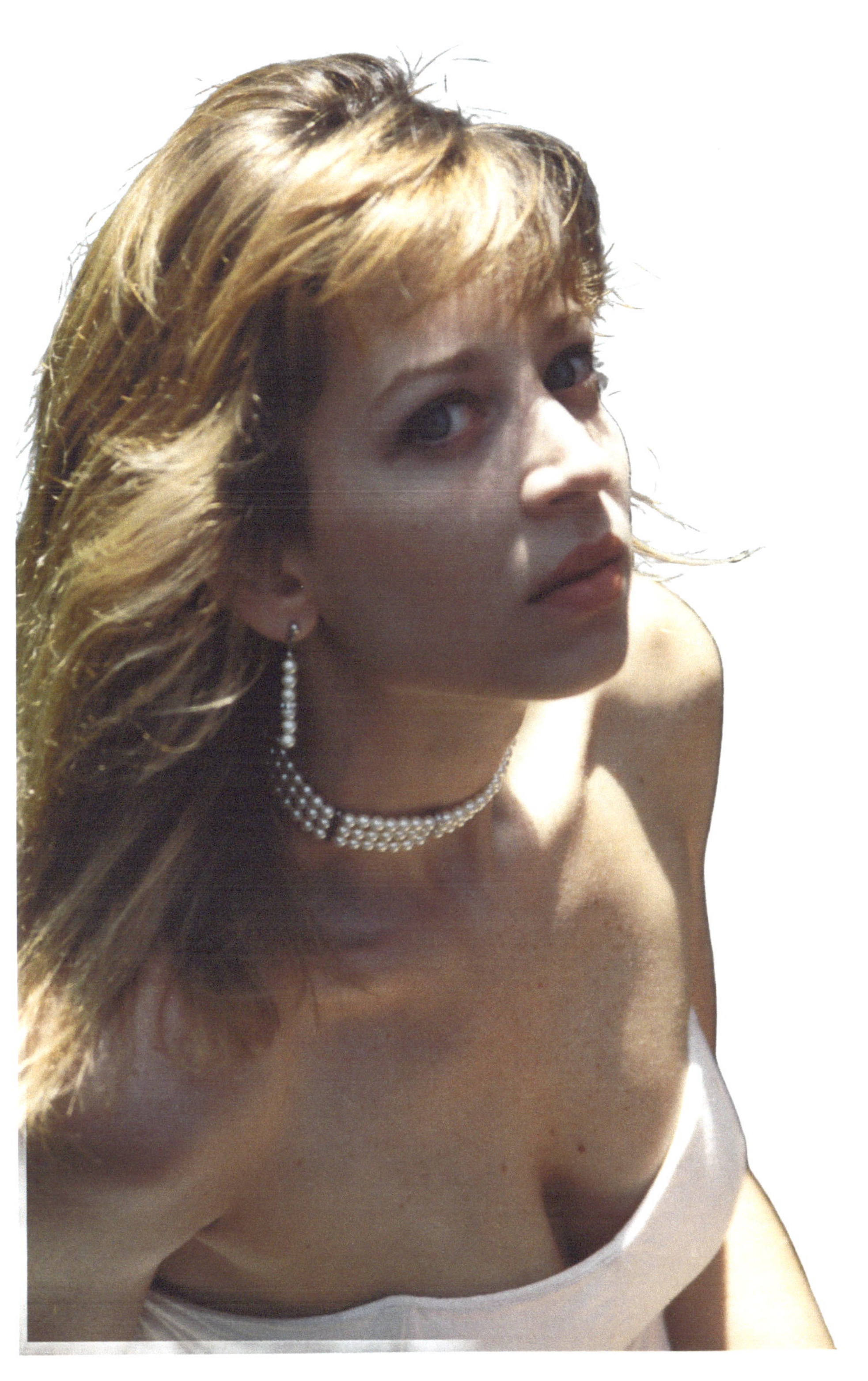
If You
Practice
SELF-LOVE
You Will
Never
Spend a Day
in Therapy

Sharon Esther Lampert

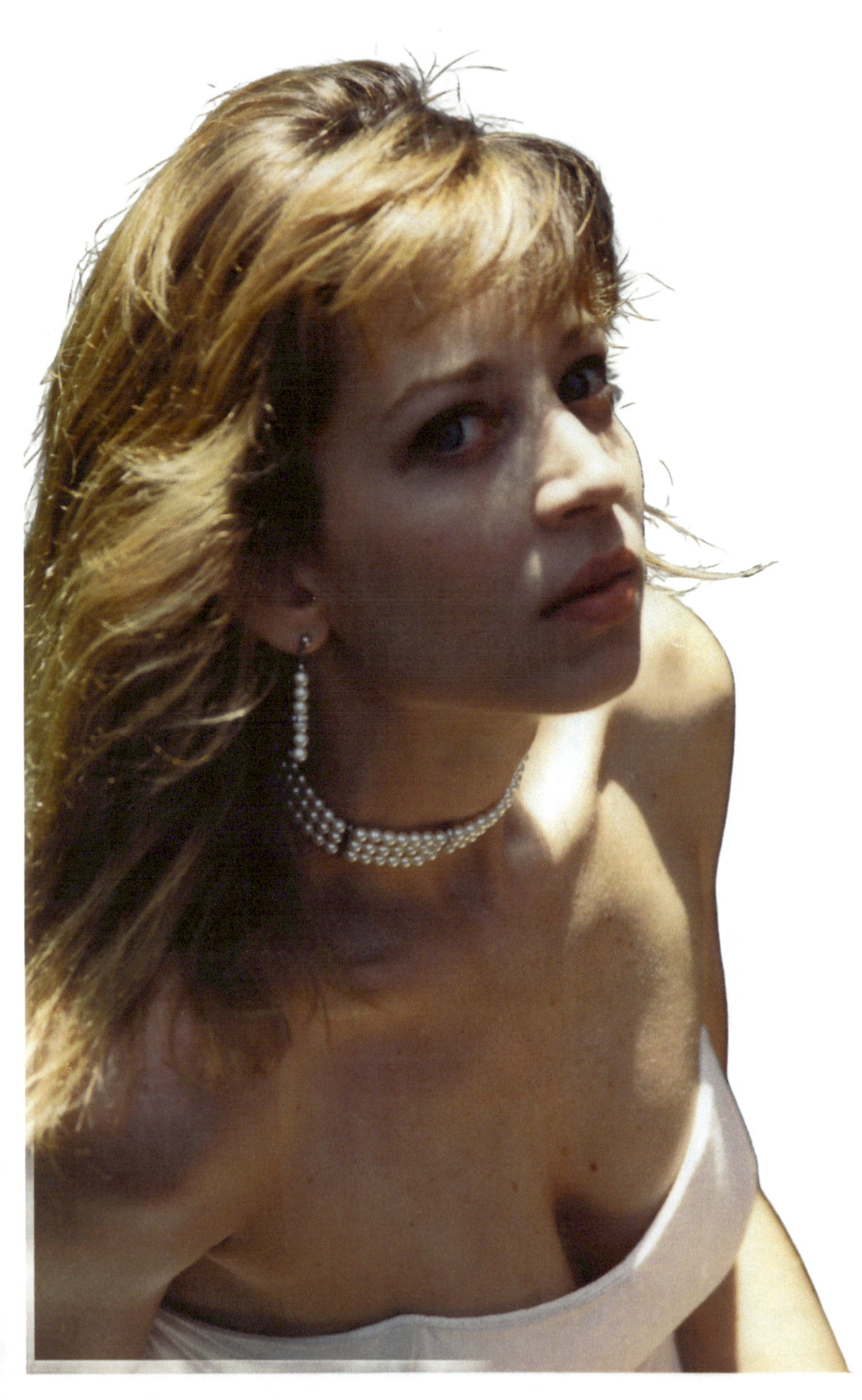

# All People **Help** You With Their **Strengths** and **Hurt** You with Their **Weaknesses**

**Sharon Esther Lampert**

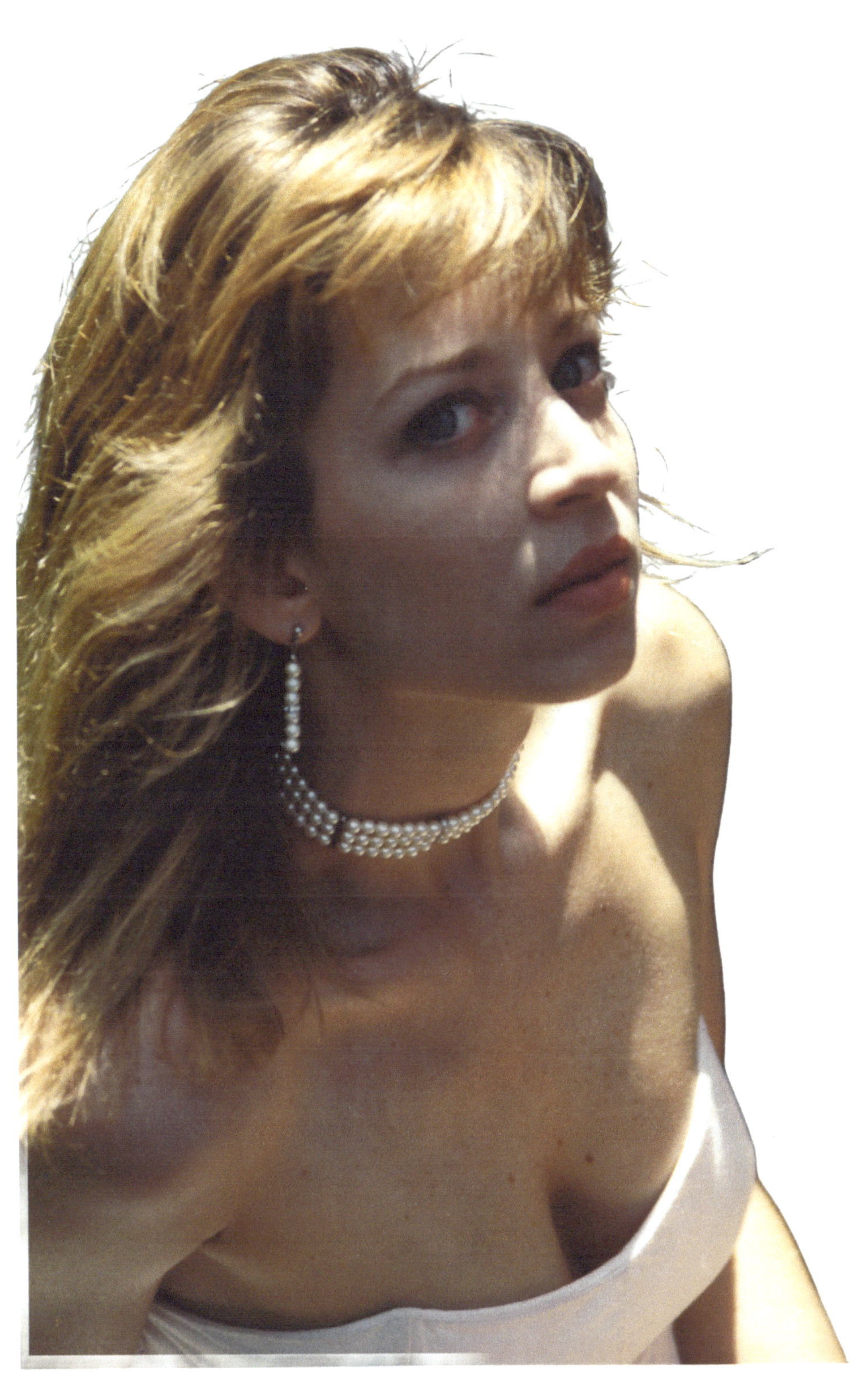

Raise Good Men
Who Love
Not Hate
Who Create
Not Destroy
Who Build
Not Bomb
Who Love
Not Screw
Sharon Esther Lampert

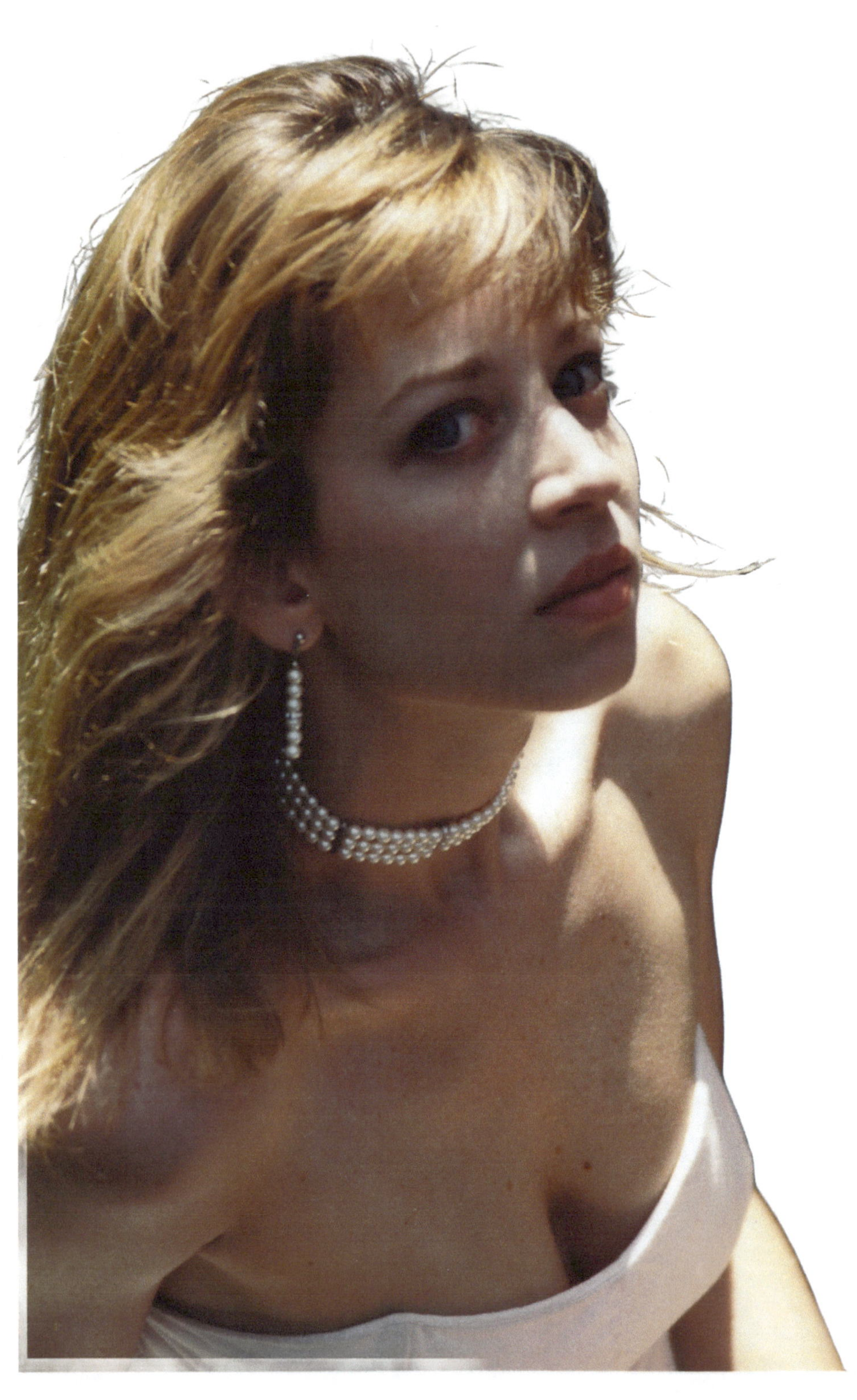
Good People
NOTHING
Is a Problem
Bad People
EVERYTHING
Is a Problem
Sharon Esther Lampert

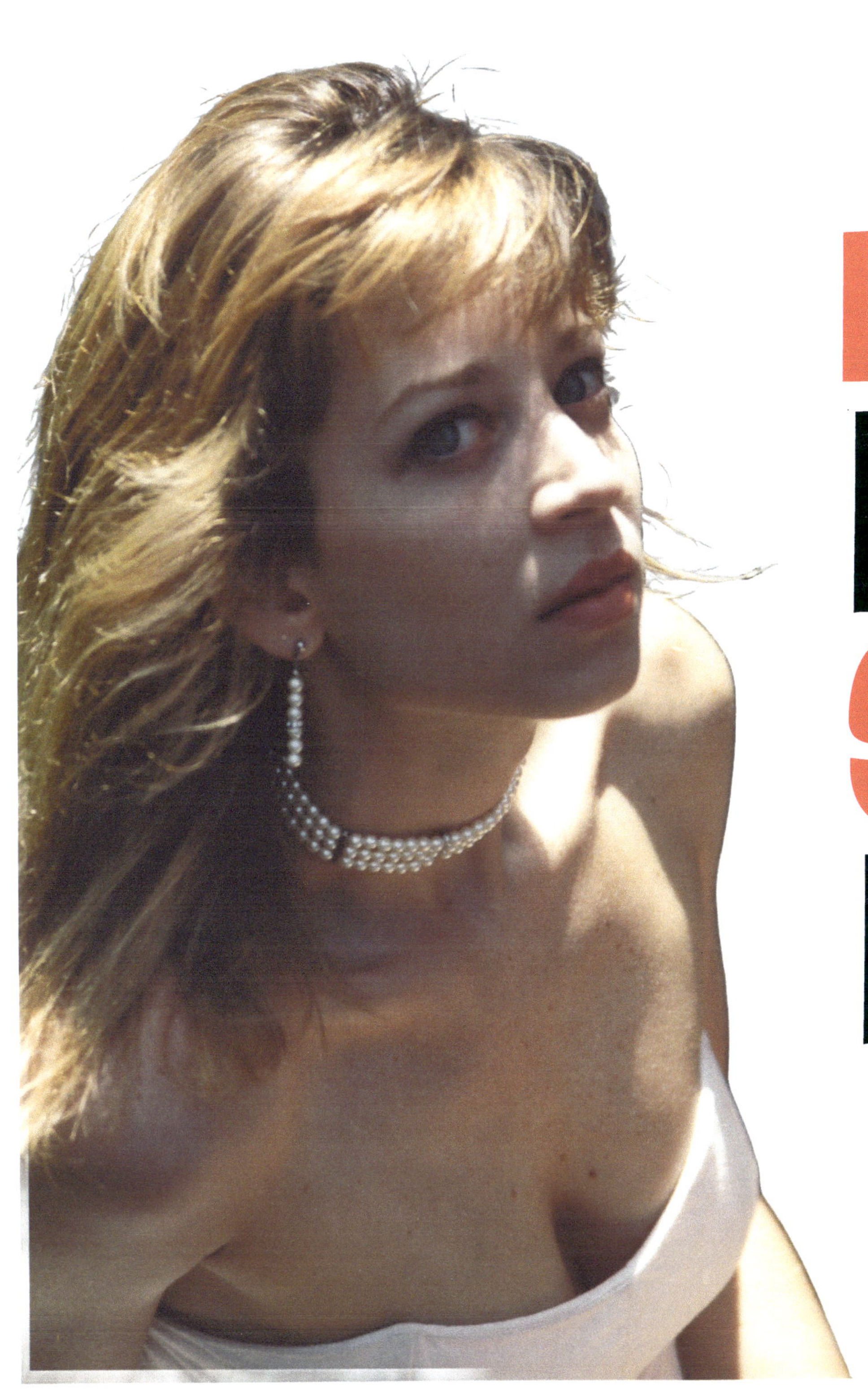LONELINESS
IS DEATH
SOLITUDE
IS DIVINE
Sharon Esther Lampert

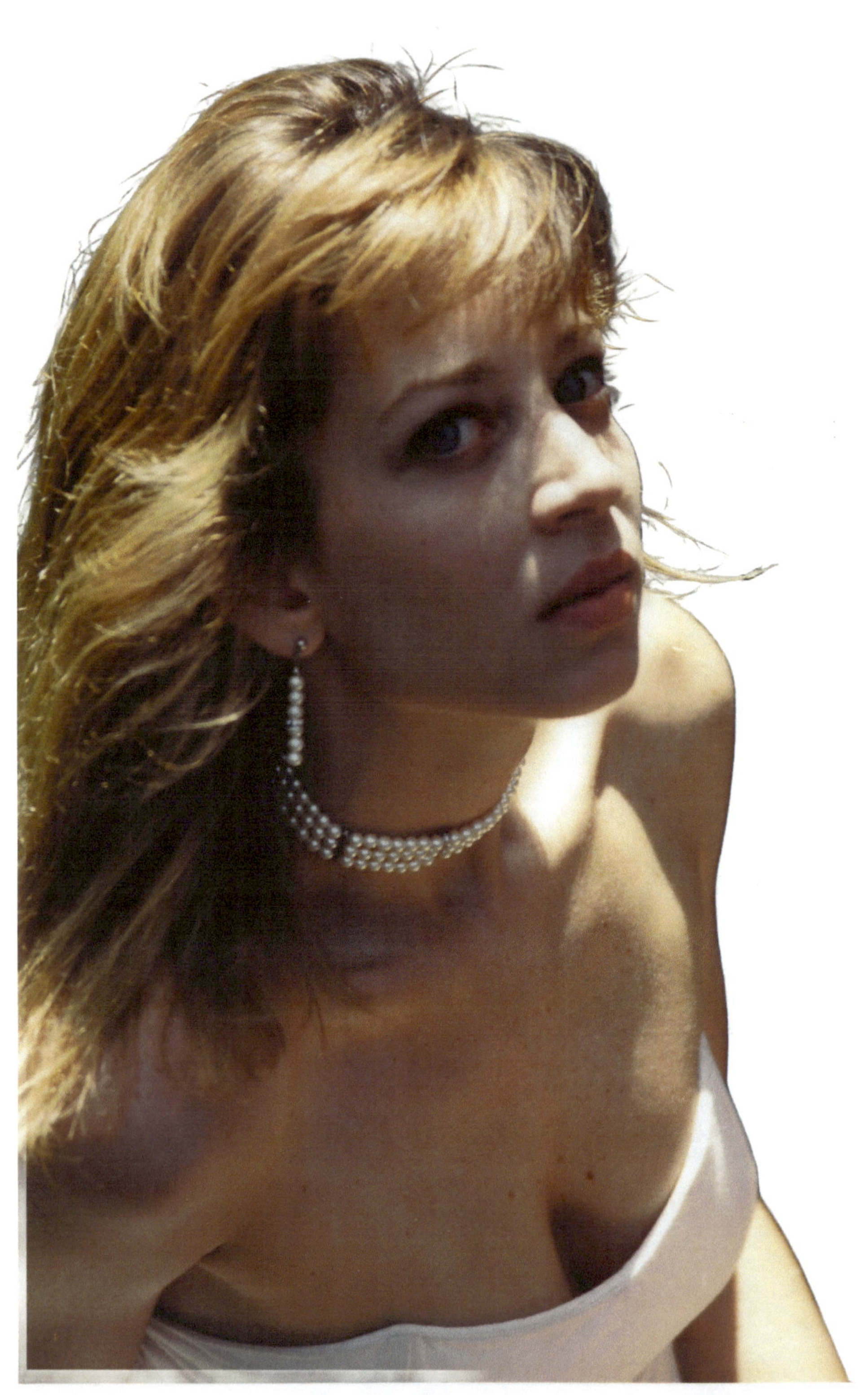

# GOT**2**GO

I am
passing
through
**LIFE**
and
**LIFE**
is passing
through me

**Sharon Esther Lampert**

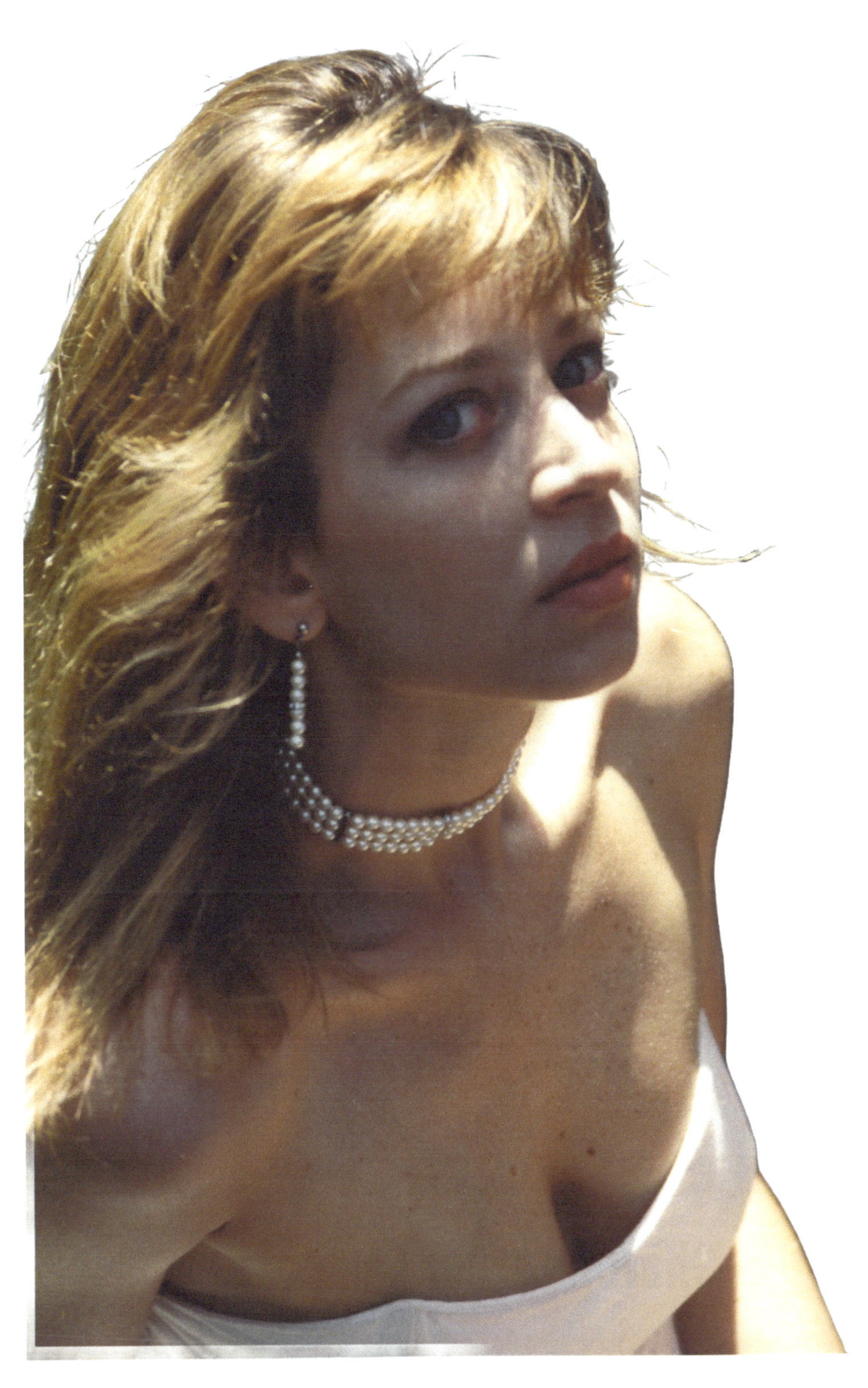

# Every WRITER Is Born with 11 Fingers; A PEN Is the 11th Appendage

**Sharon Esther Lampert**

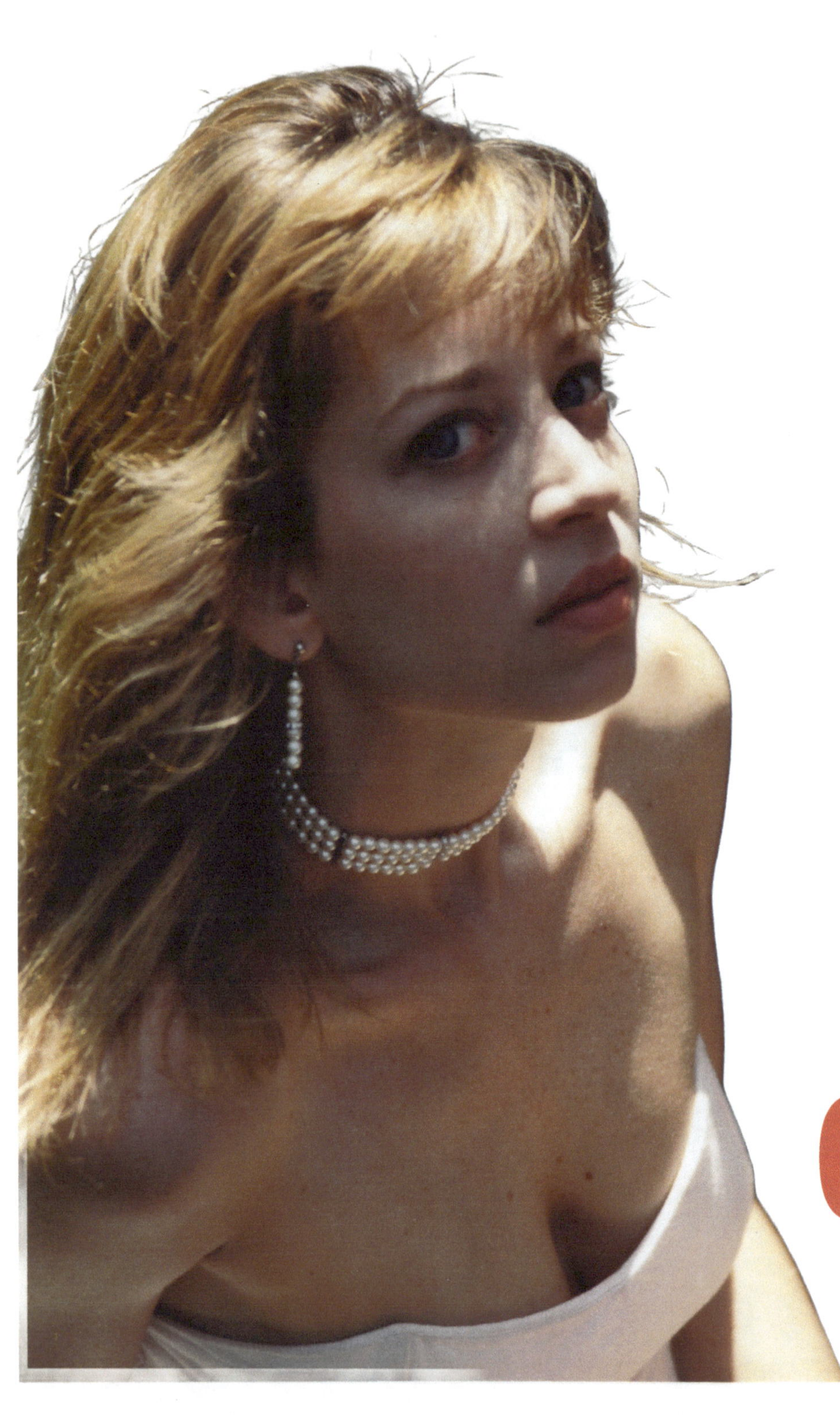

# THE FINE LINE BETWEEN GENIUS AND INSANITY IS ORGANIZATION

**Sharon Esther Lampert**

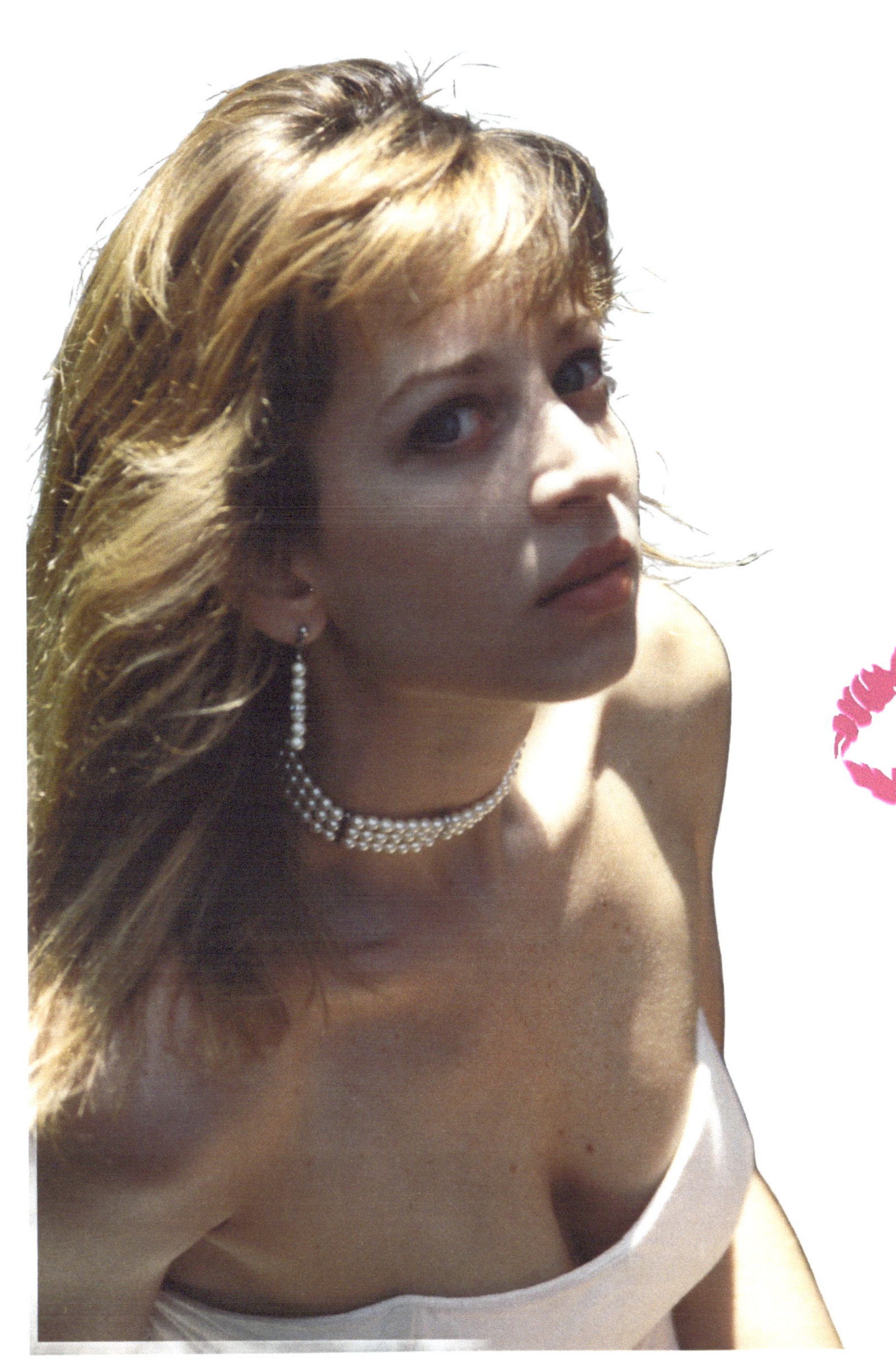

Do you
want me
to sign it
in
**INK**
or
in
**LIPSTICK?**

Sharon Esther Lampert

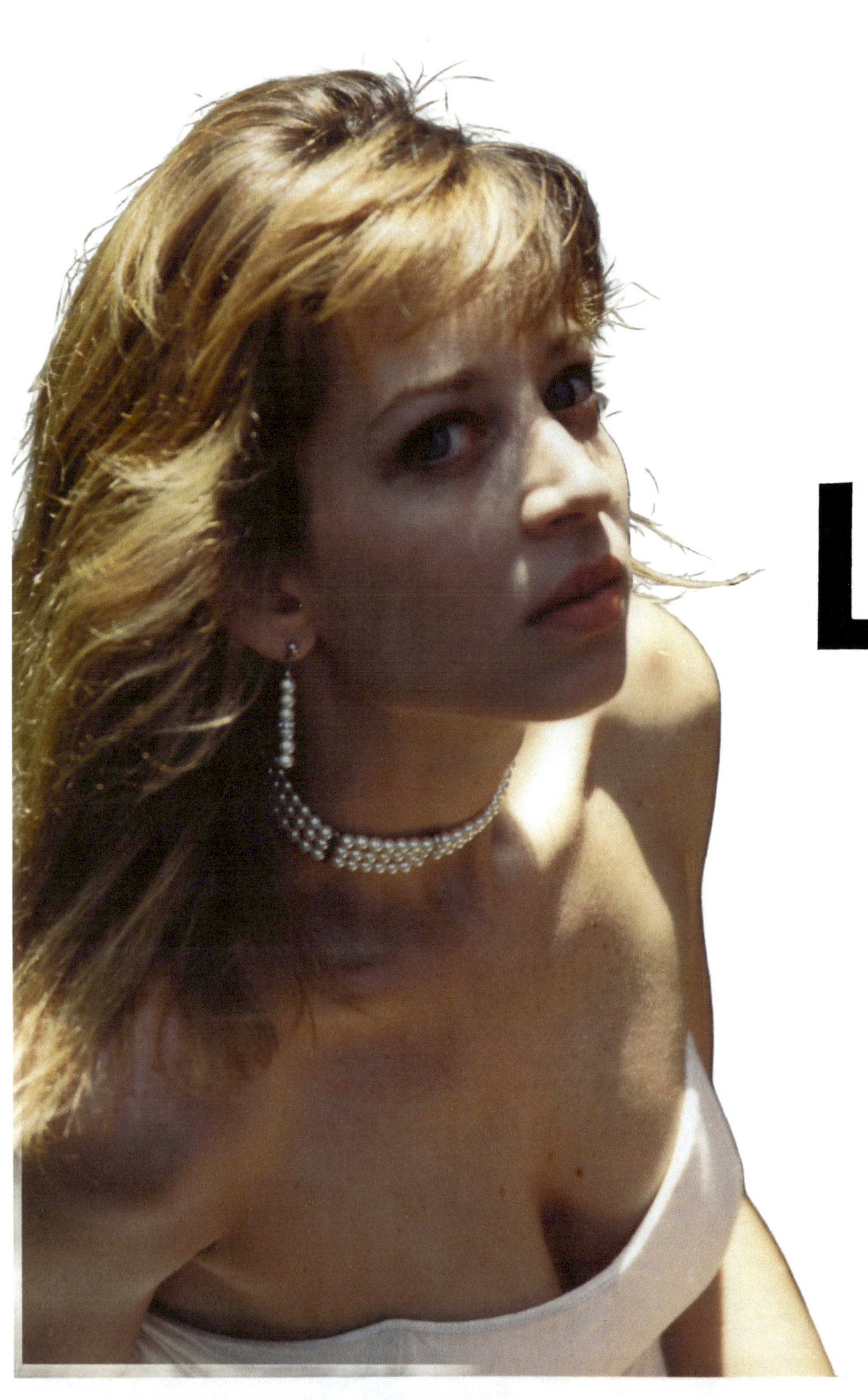
KEEP
THEM
LAUGHING
KEEP
THEM
SANE

Sharon Esther Lampert

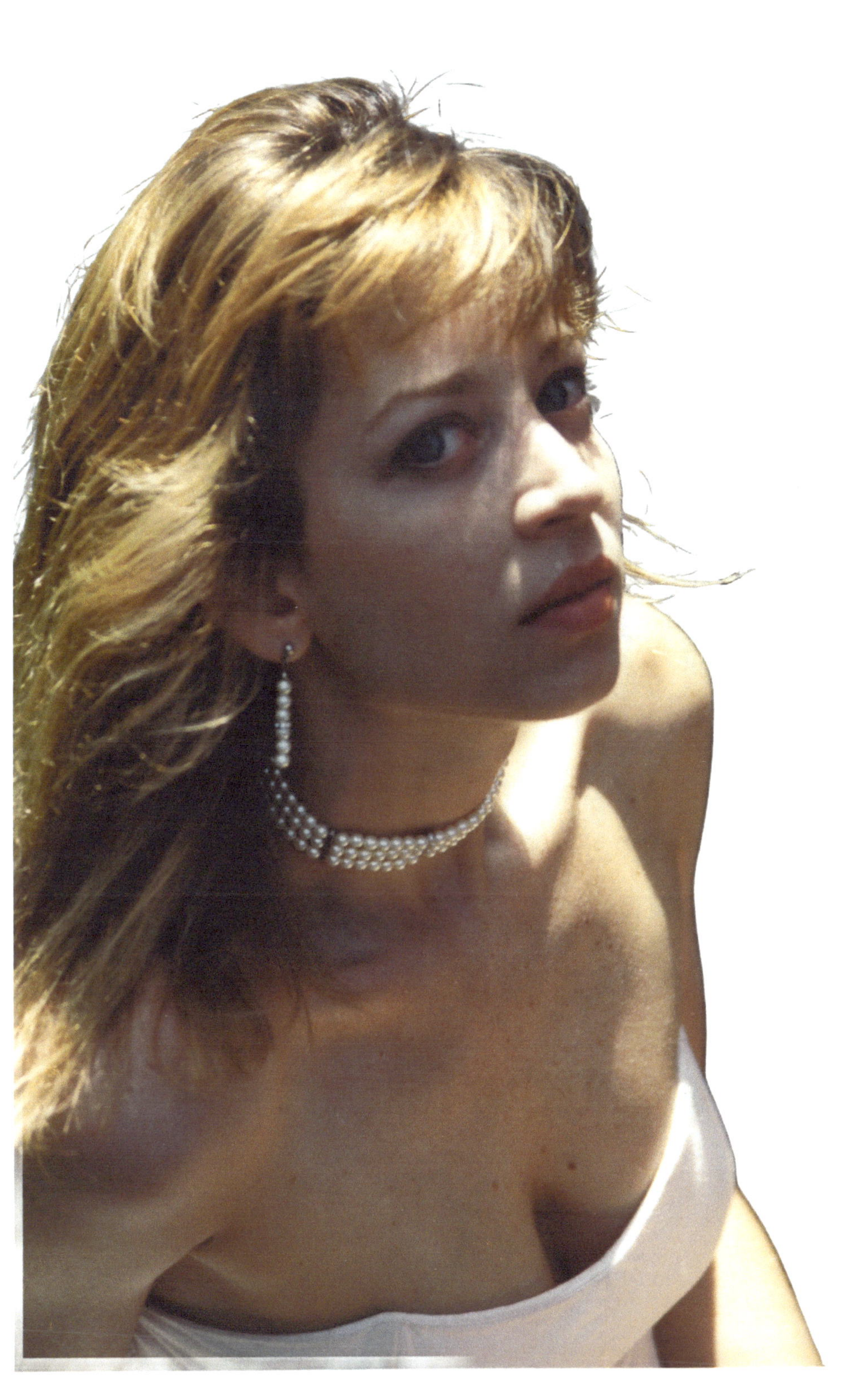

A
WARM
NOBODY
IS
BETTER
THAN A
COLD
SOMEBODY
Sharon Esther Lampert

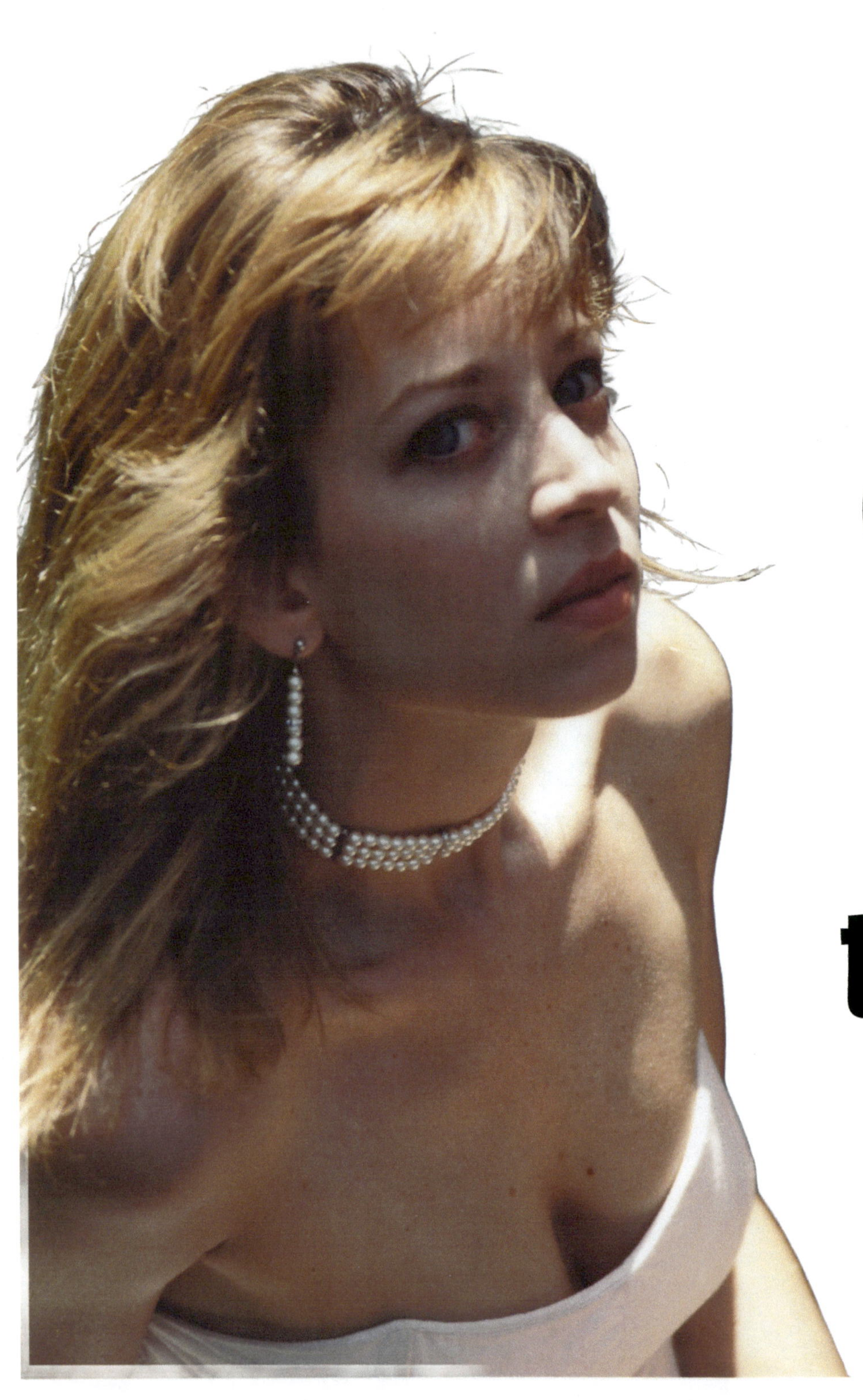
Are you making conversation or are you giving me the business?
Sharon Esther Lampert

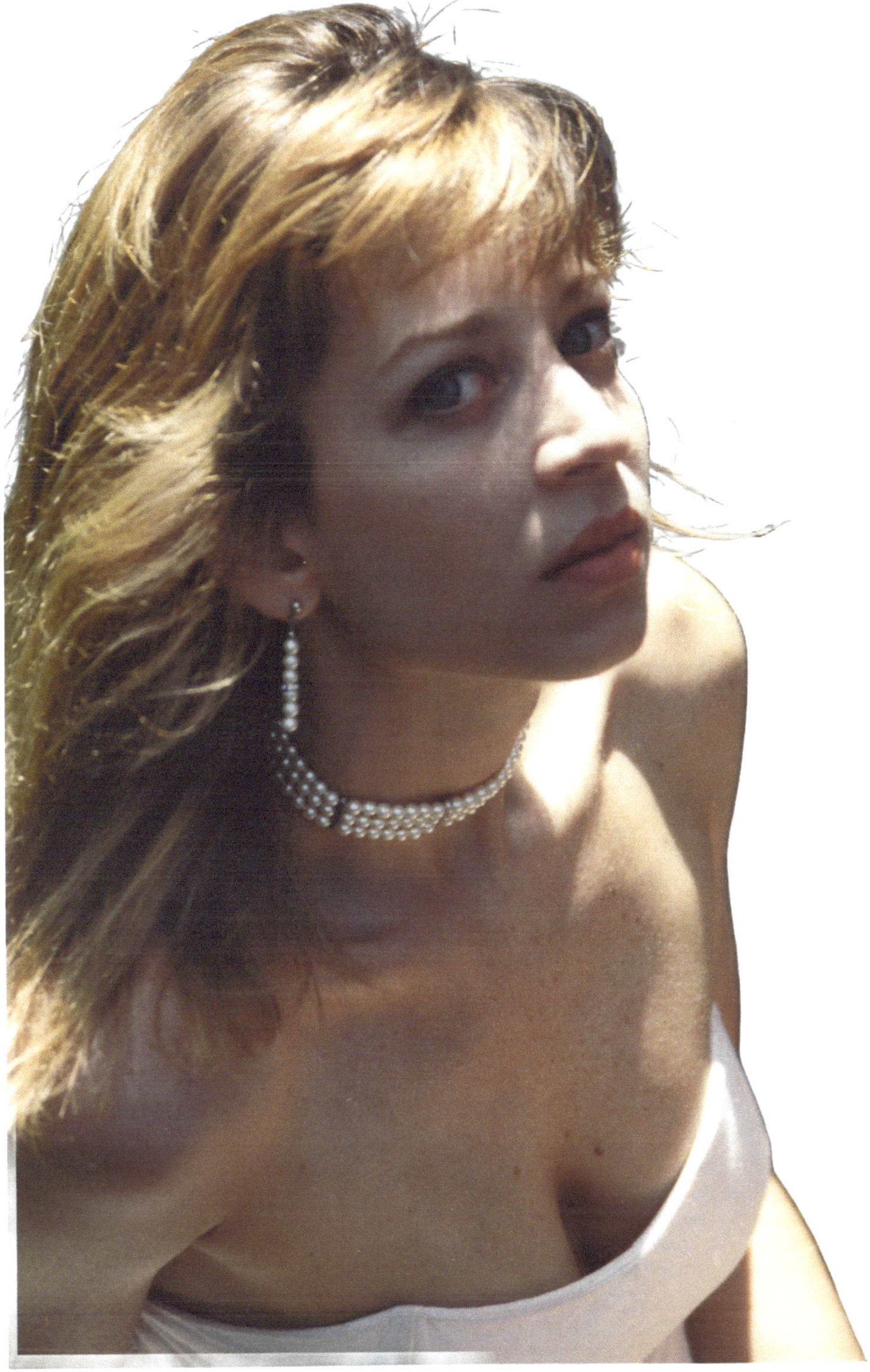

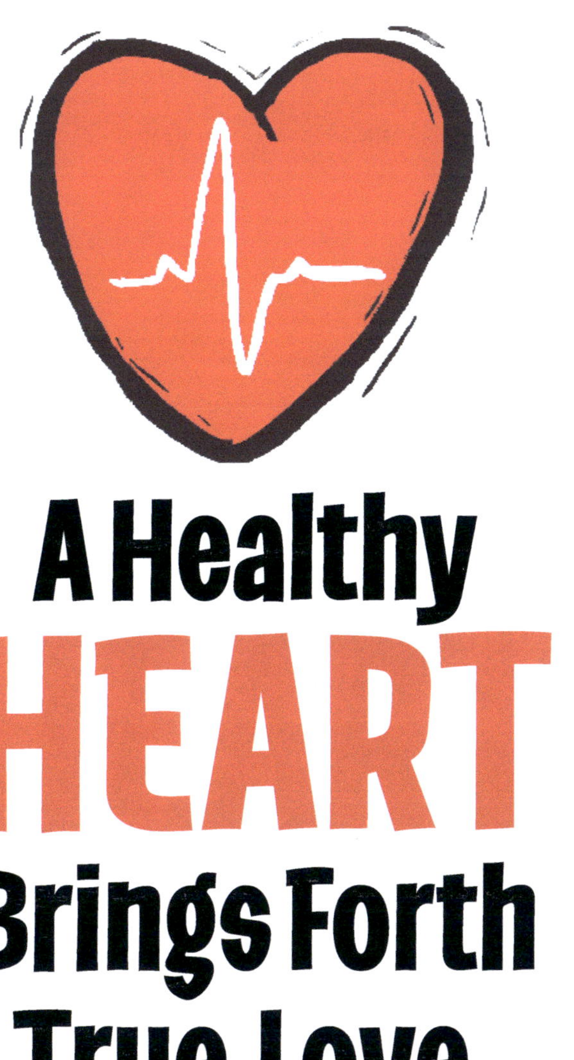

# A Healthy HEART Brings Forth True Love, Real Friends, and Long Life!

Sharon Esther Lampert

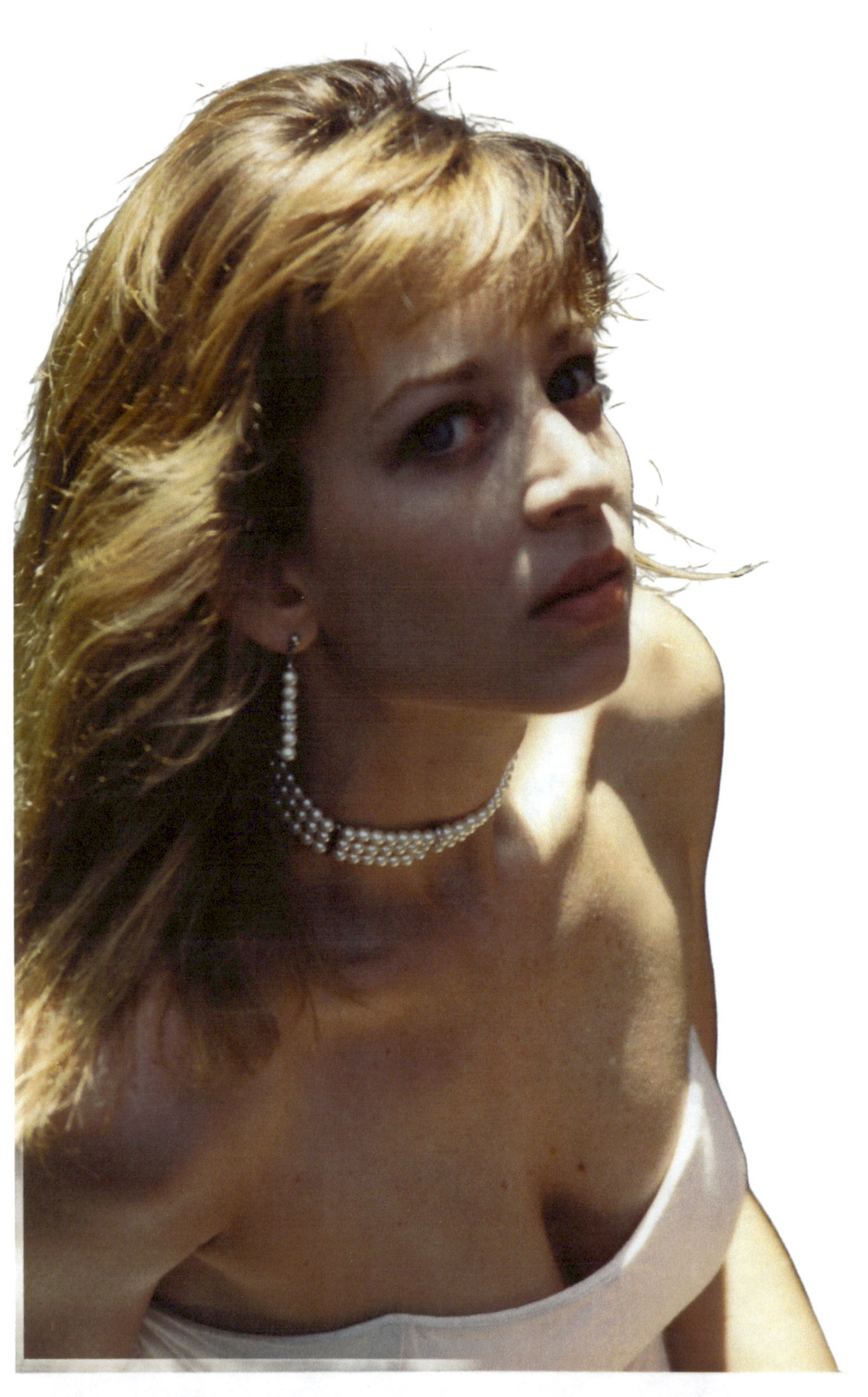

# Think
# Things
# Through
# Take
# Action
# Move
# Forward

## Sharon Esther Lampert

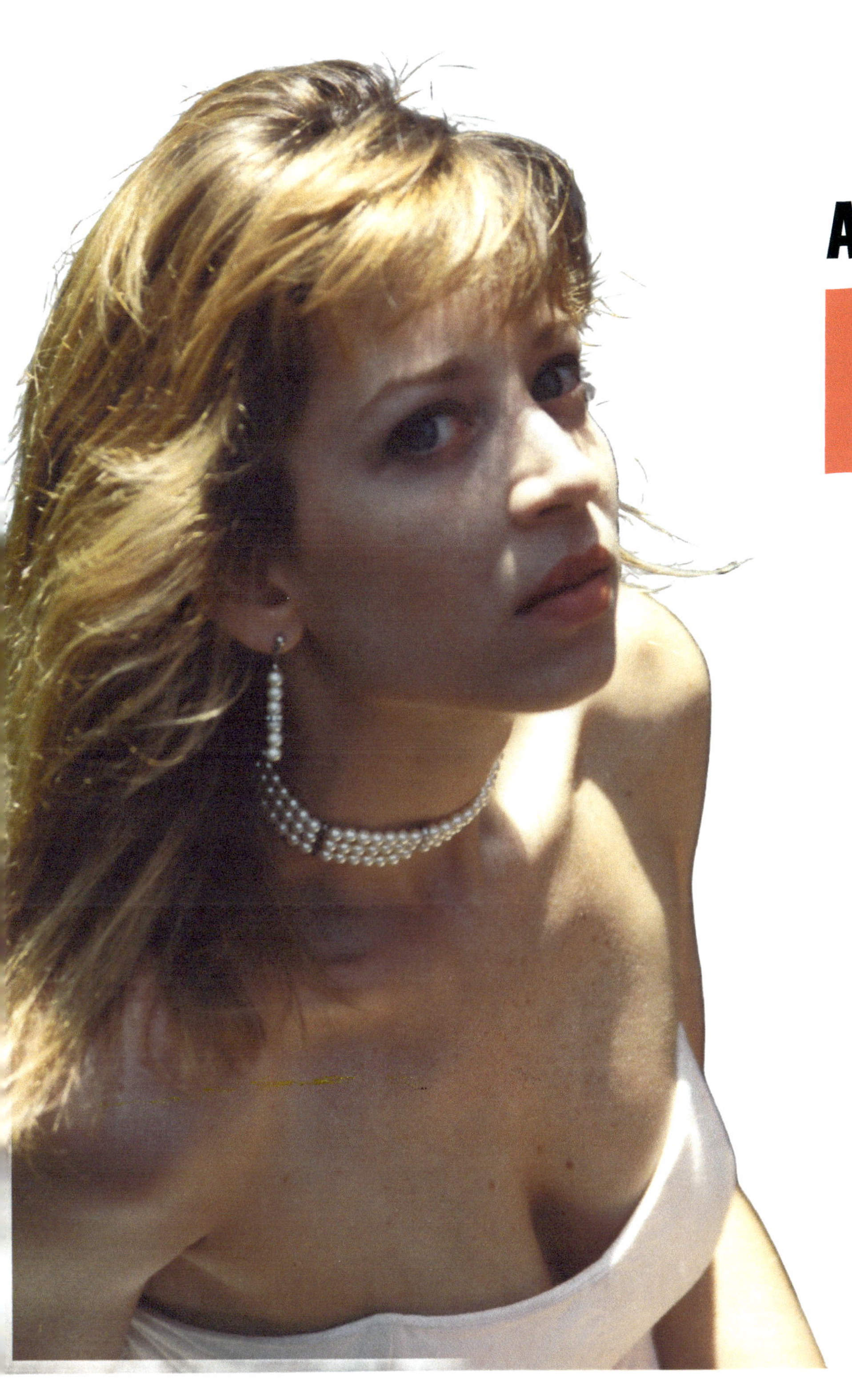

# All You Get For NEGATIVITY Is NOTHING

## Sharon Esther Lampert

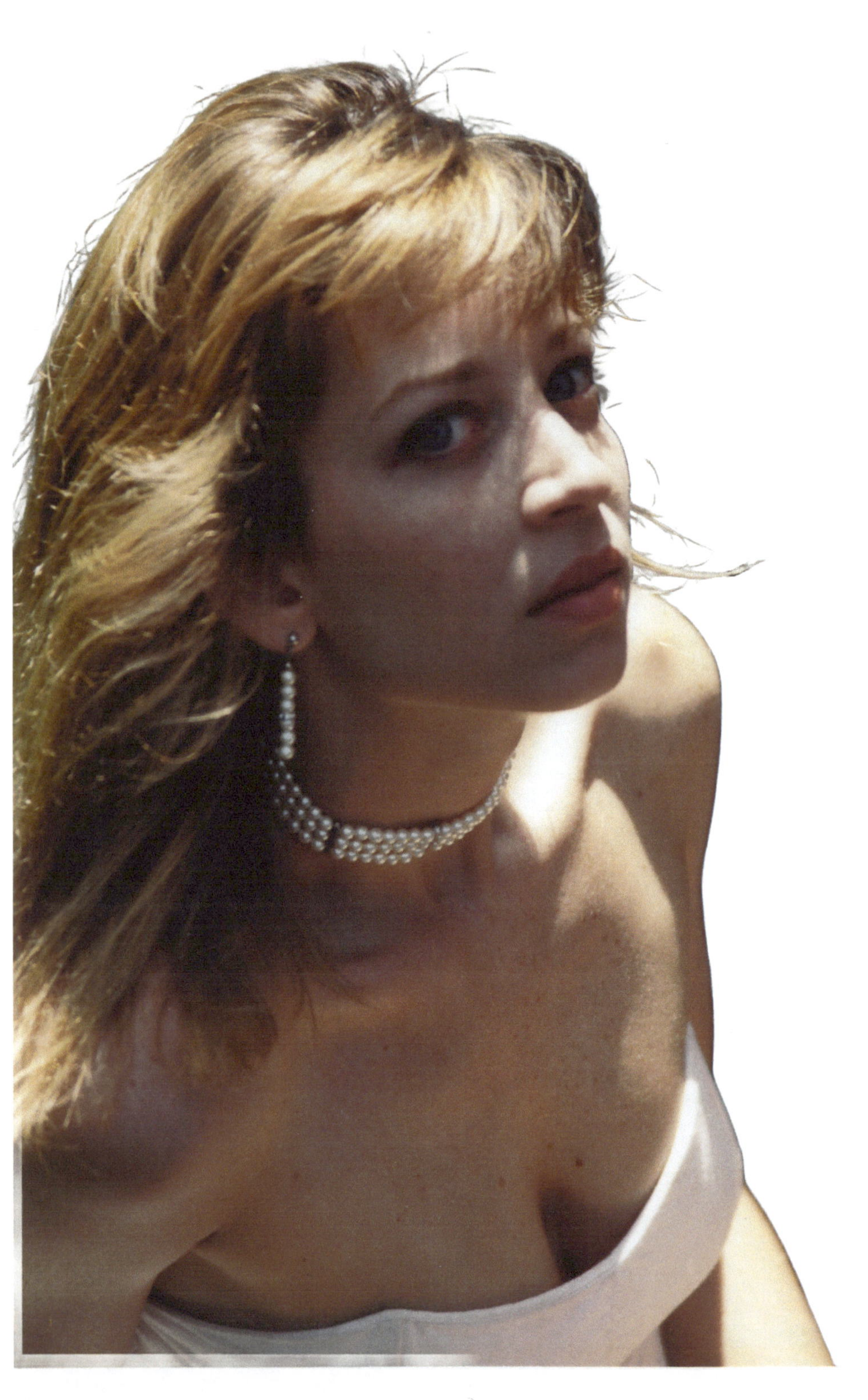

# I Don't Do Reality

**Sharon Esther Lampert**

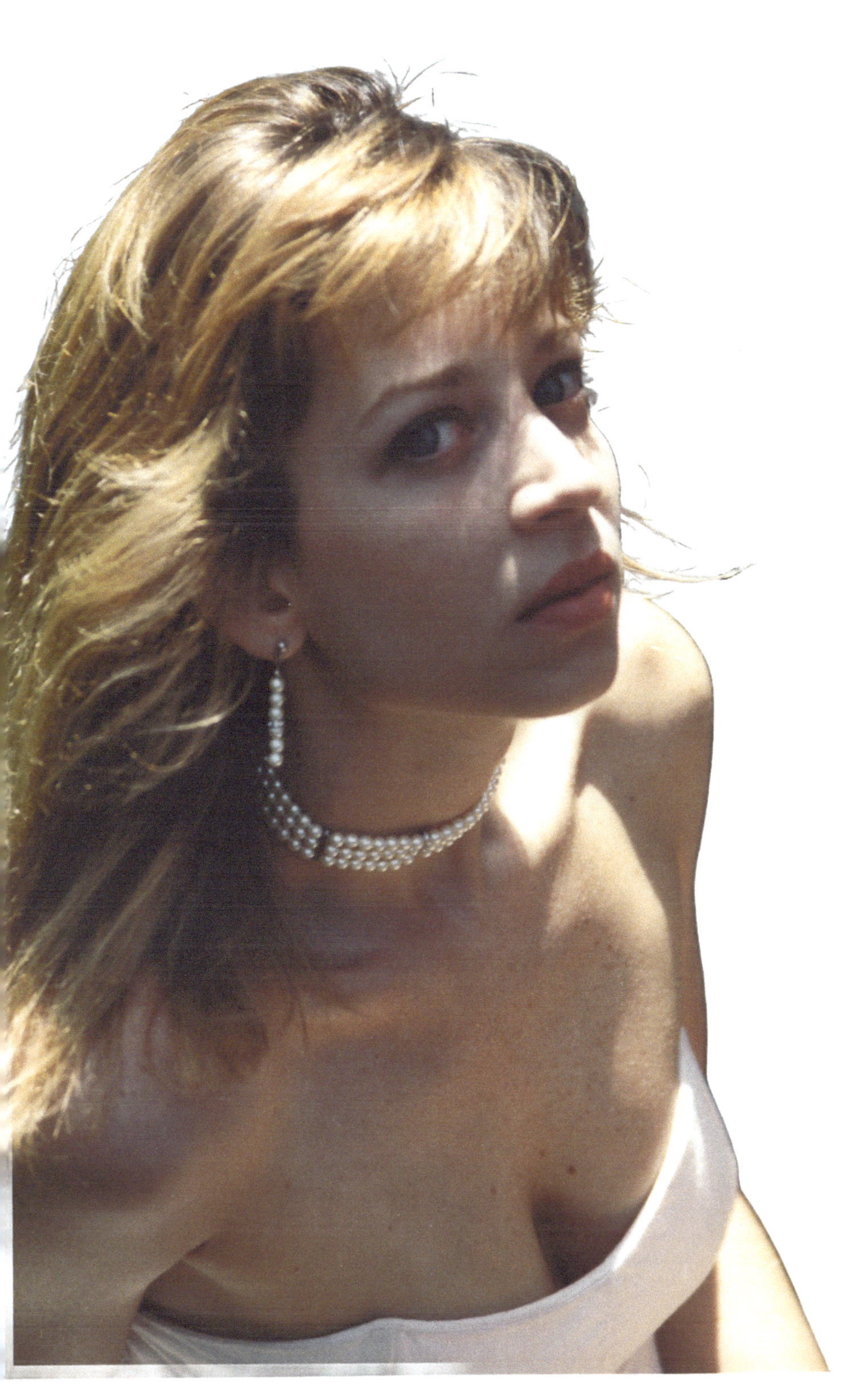

# NORMAL IS TOO HARD

## Sharon Esther Lampert

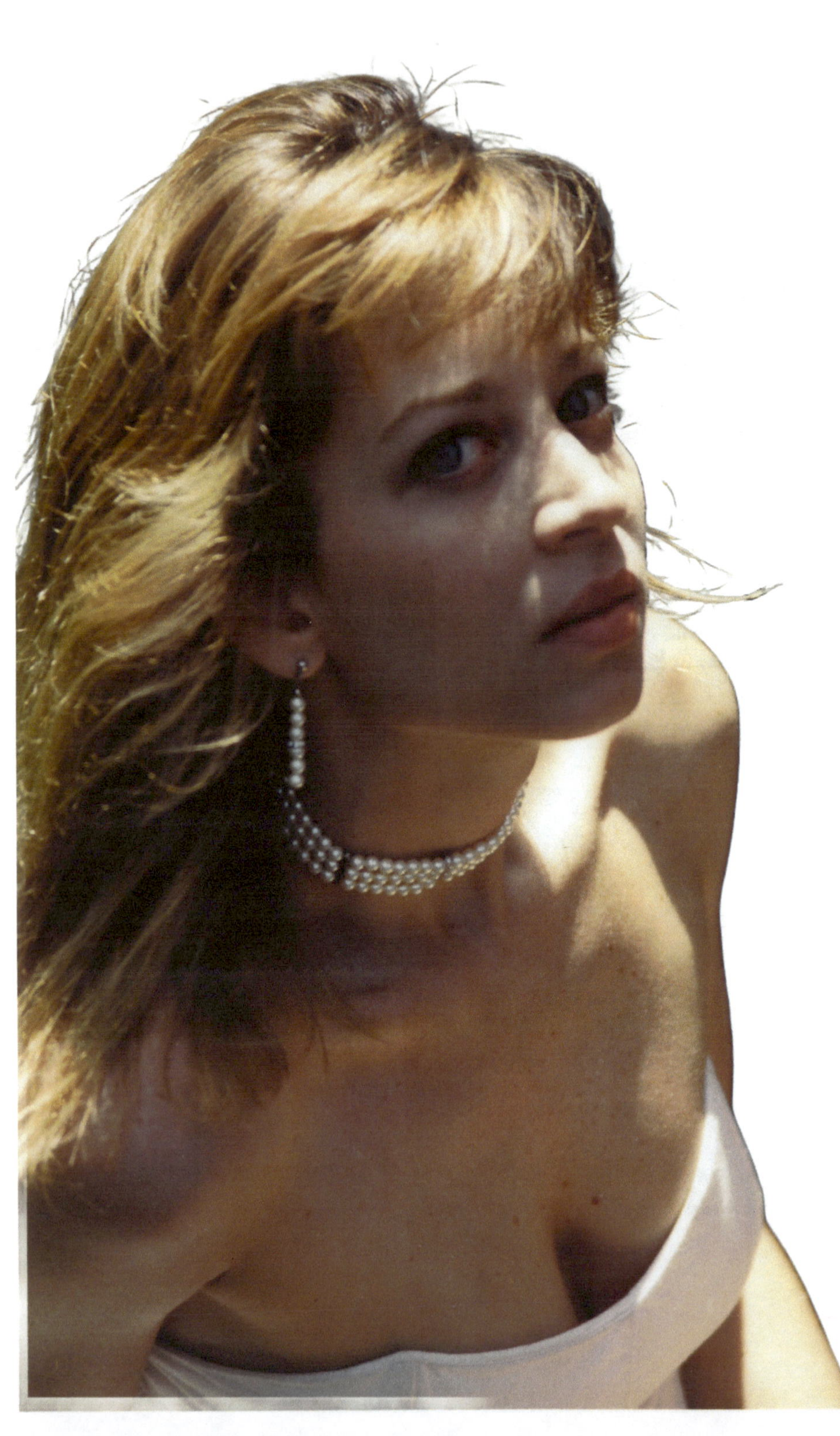

WIN
WHAT'S IMPORTANT NOW!
Sharon Esther Lampert

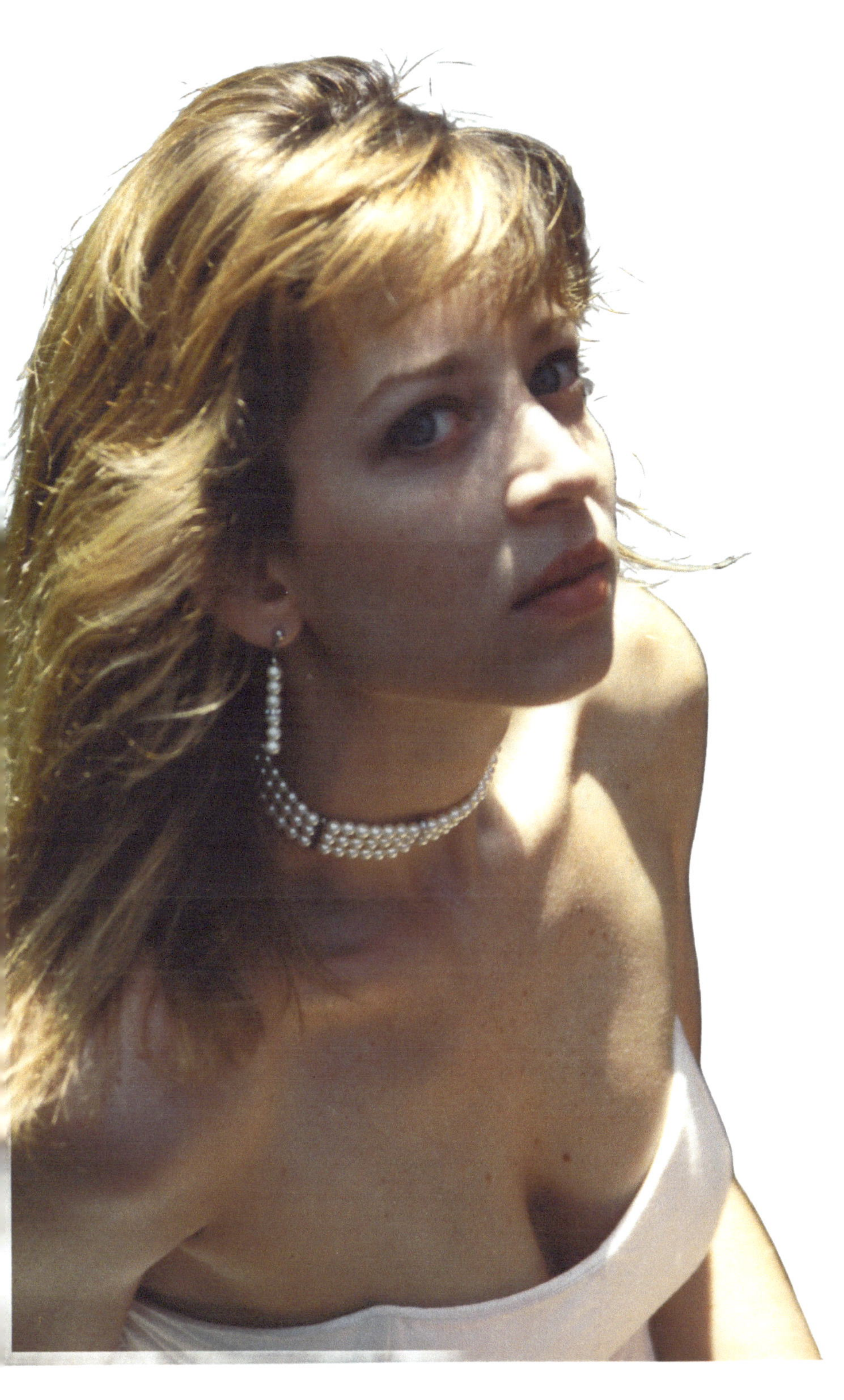

# UNLEASH THE CREATOR THE GOD WITHIN

## Sharon Esther Lampert

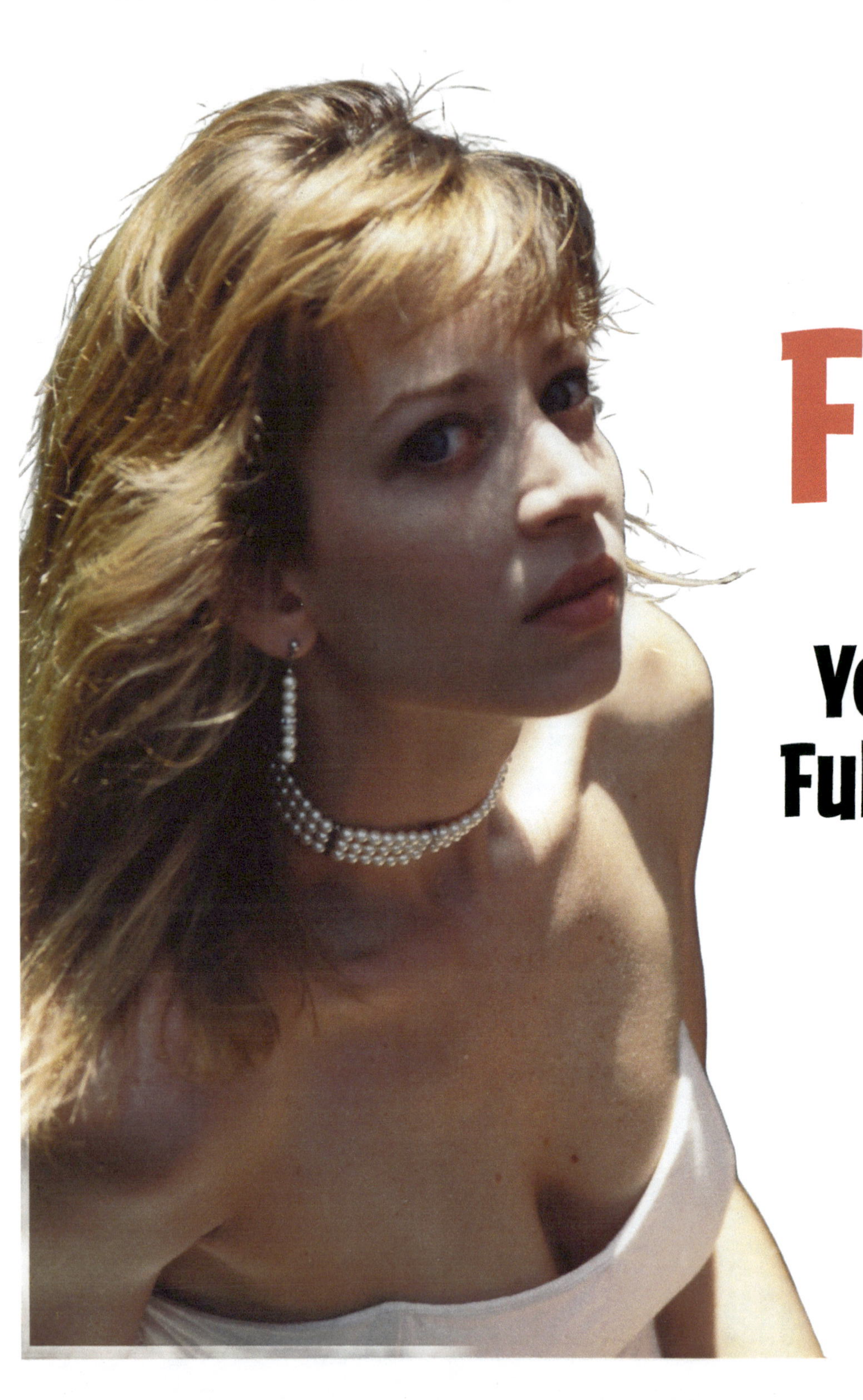

# FEMINISM

## Freedom to Chart Your Own Destiny and Fulfill Your Own Dreams

### Sharon Esther Lampert

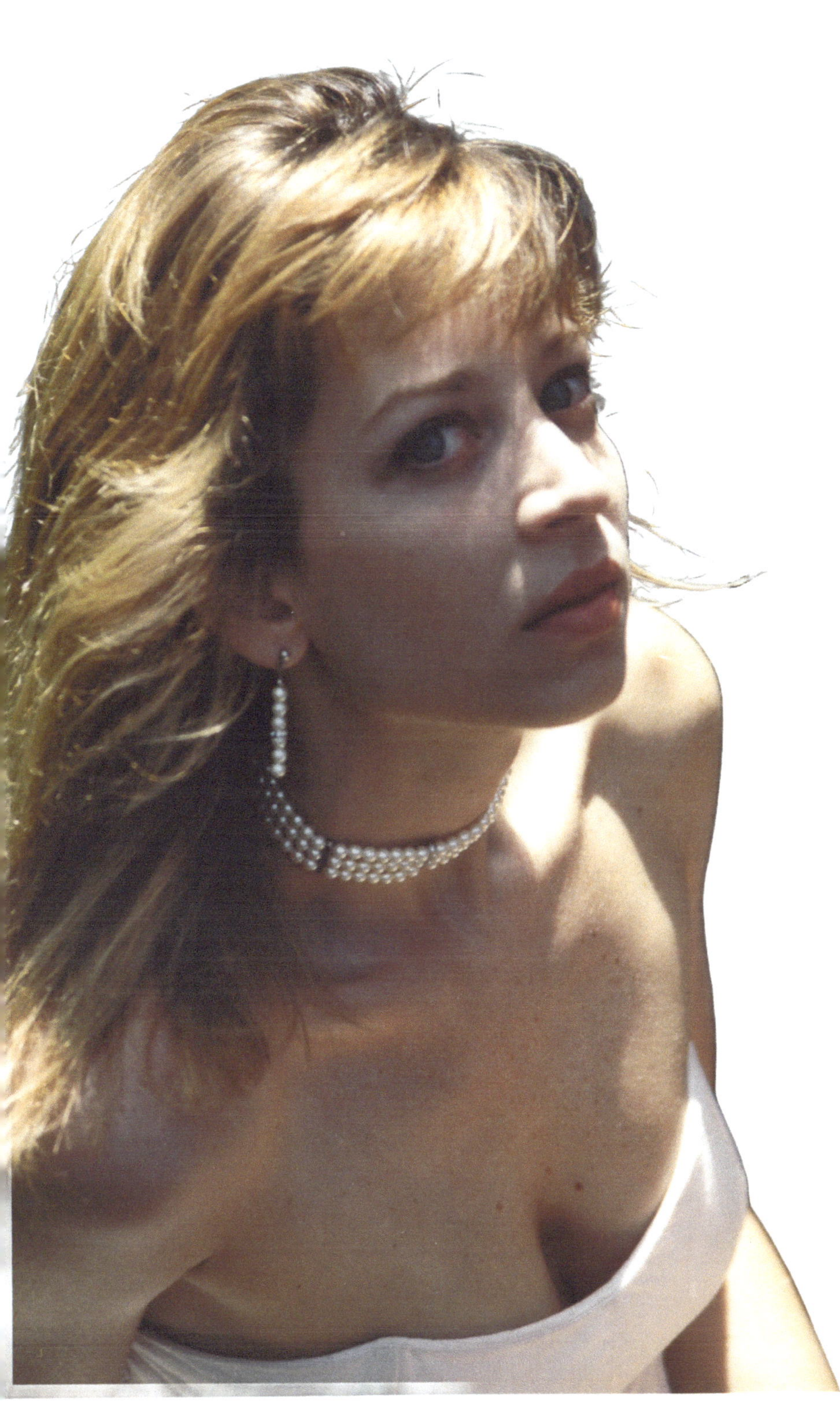

# WOMAN HAVE ALL THE POWER

## But Have Never Learned How to Use It

### Sharon Esther Lampert

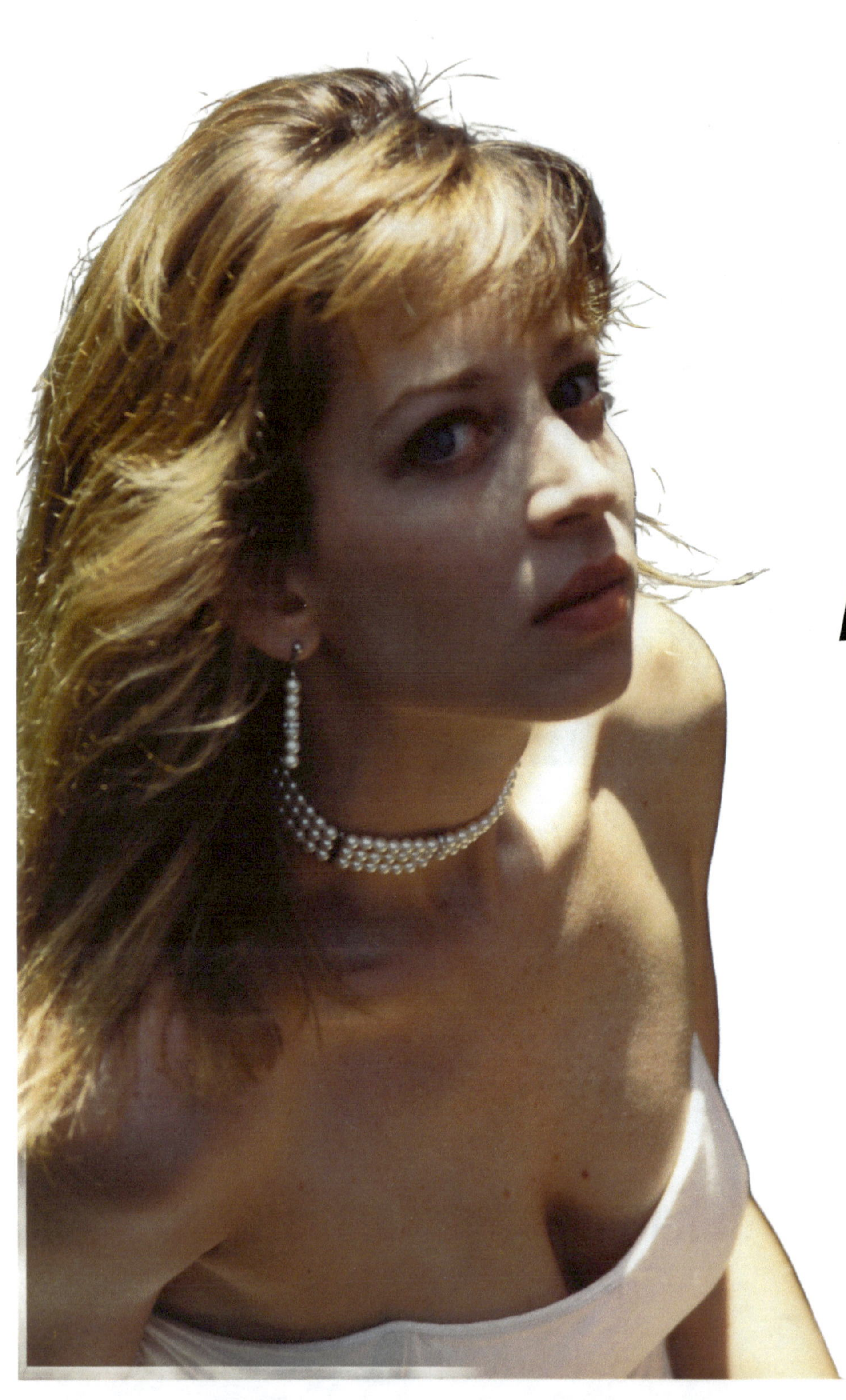

# Education Cannot Amerliorate Anti-Semitism Haters Hate the Facts, the Truth, and the Light

**Sharon Esther Lampert**

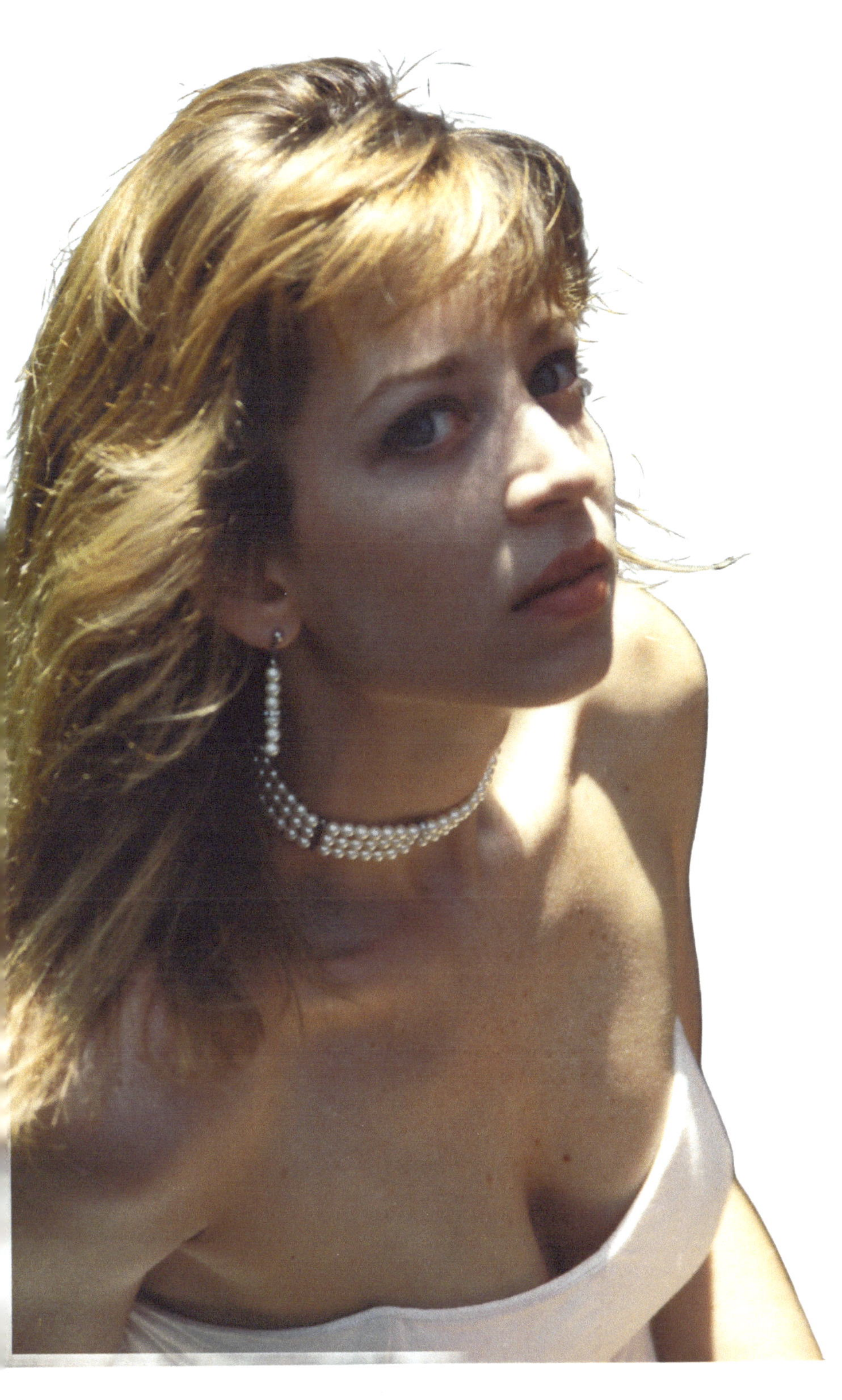

# You Cannot Negotiate with Evil. Destroy the Evil or be Destroyed by the Evil.

**Sharon Esther Lampert**

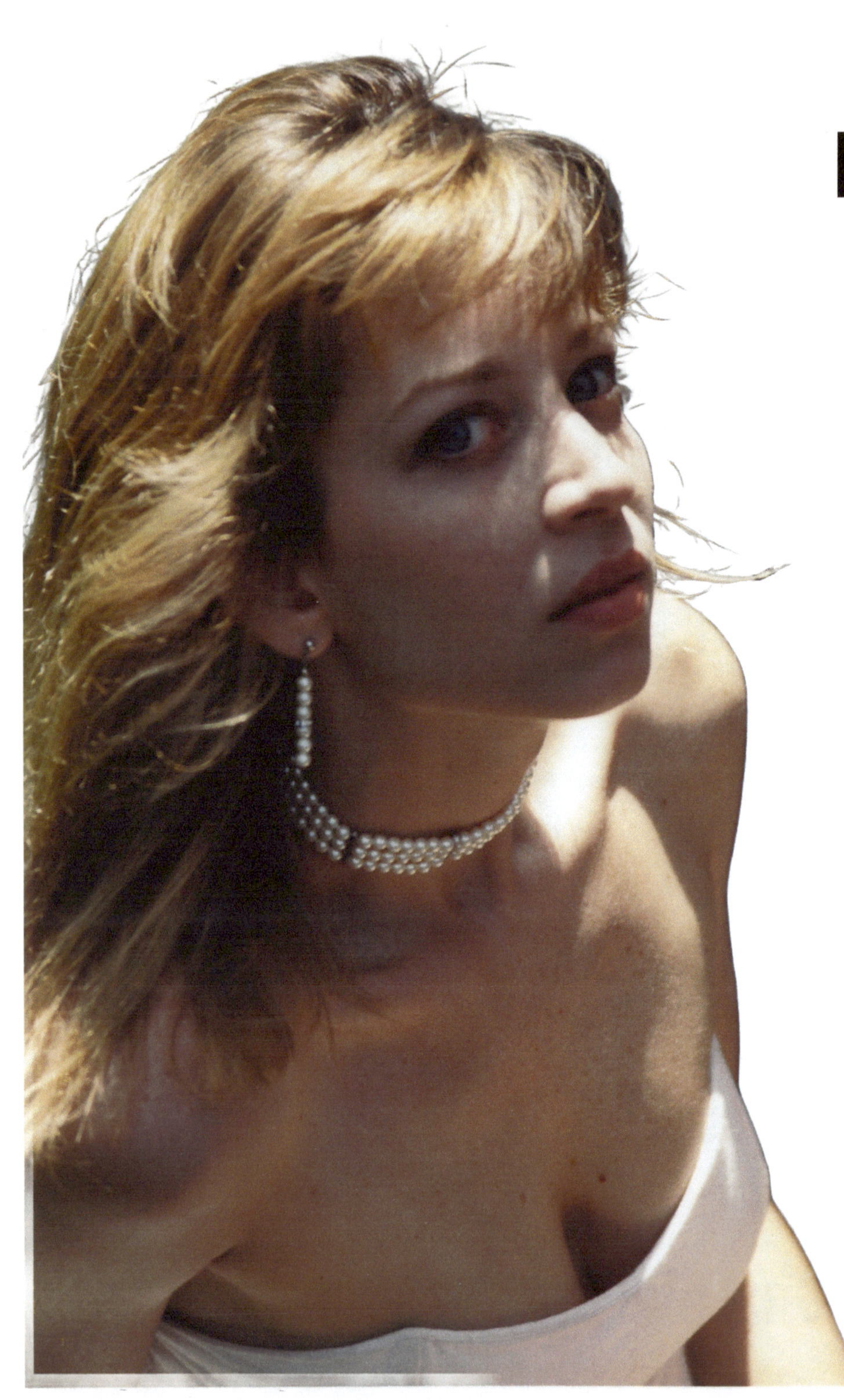

# I AM A PROPHET

I deliver the message
What you do with
the message is
your business!

Sharon Esther Lampert

## PRINCESS KADIMAH
### 8TH PROPHETESS OF ISRAEL

## GOD IS GO! DO!
### THE 22 COMMANDMENTS

# GOD IS GO! DO!

1. THERE ARE TWO WORLDS:
A PHYSICAL WORLD AND A **METAPHYSICAL** WORLD

2. GOD IS NOT PHYSICS THE LAWS OF THE UNIVERSE
**GOD IS METAPHYSICS**

3. YOUR MIND, THOUGHTS, AND IDEAS ARE **INVISIBLE** AND **INTANGIBLE** ENTITIES
— BEYOND THE SCOPE OF SCIENTIFIC INQUIRY!

4. **GOD IS GO! DO!**
**GOD CAN ONLY DO FOR YOU WHAT GOD CAN DO THROUGH YOU**

5. **PRAY** AS IF IT ALL DEPENDS ON GOD!
**WORK** AS IF IT ALL DEPENDS ON YOU!

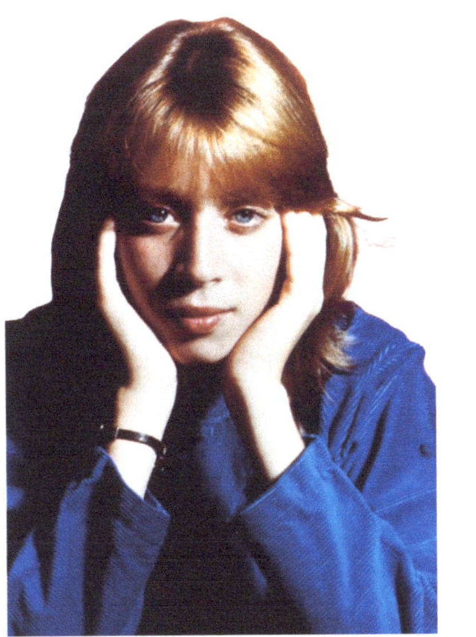

**THE 22 COMMANDMENTS**
**UNIVERSAL MORAL COMPASS**
**YOU HAD TO OUTDO MOSES!**

Prophet Sharon Esther Lampert

# WORLD PEACE EQUATION

## VG+VL=VP

Virtue of the Good + Value of Life = Vision of Peace

The Mathematical and
Philosophical Proof for World Peace

$$VG + VL = VP$$

$$VP = VG + VL$$

$$VP = V(G+L)$$

$$P = (G+L)$$

Peace = Good + Life

Peace = Good Life

www.WorldPeaceEquation.com

Sharon Esther Lampert

A WRITER IS AN ARTIST WHO PAINTS WITH WORDS

Sharon Esther Lampert

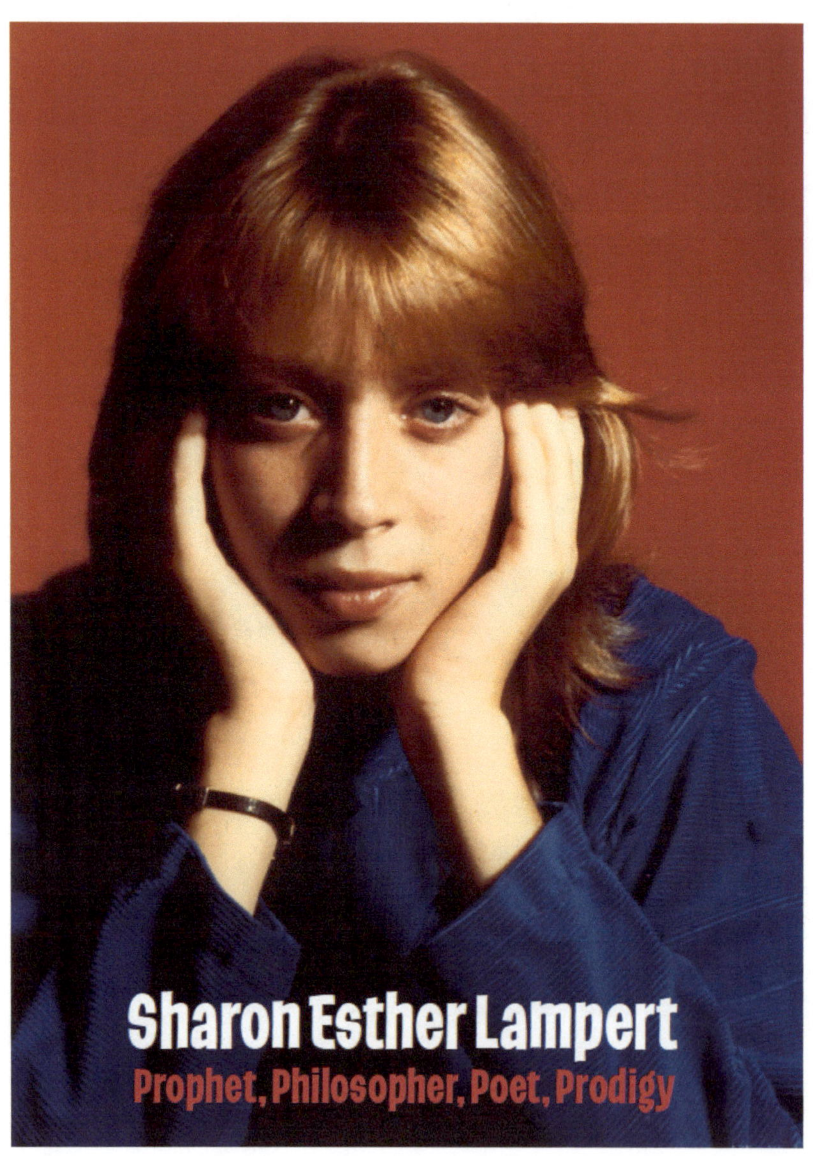


NO **FAKES**
NO **FLOPS**
NO **FILLER**
NO **FLUFF**
NO **FUDGE**
NO **FAT**
NO **F-BOMB**

©SharonEstherLampert.com

# TRUE LOVE

True Love Is Unconditional
True Love Is Found in the Deed
True Love Is Found in the We
True Love Joins the Heart
Mind, and Body as One

Sharon Esther Lampert

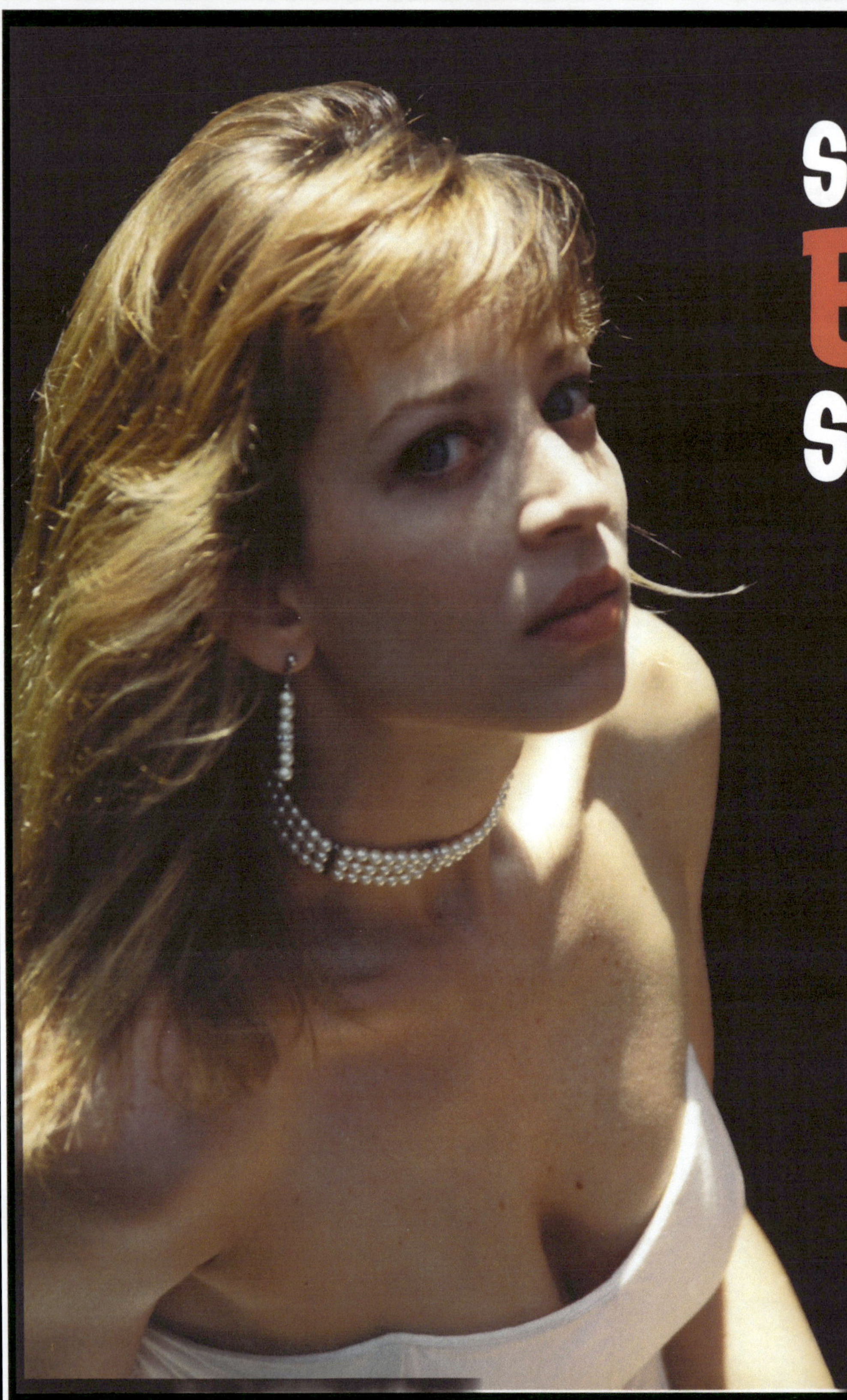
Solve One Problem
EDUCATION
Save Entire World

SHARON
ESTHER
LAMPERT

SMARTGRADES
BRAIN POWER REVOLUTION

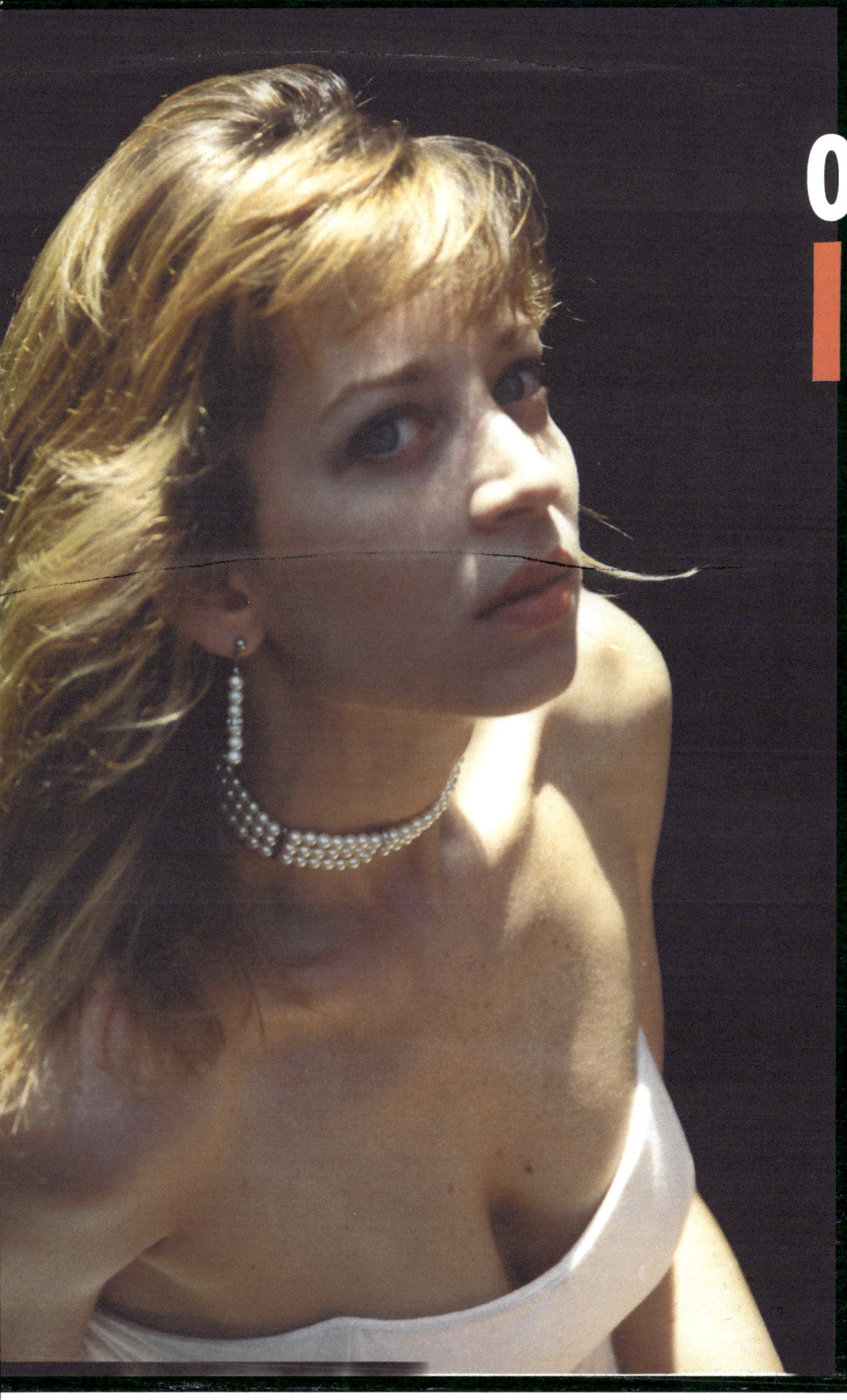
ONE GLOBAL ENEMY
IGNORANCE
SHARON
ESTHER
LAMPERT
SMARTGRADES
BRAIN POWER REVOLUTION

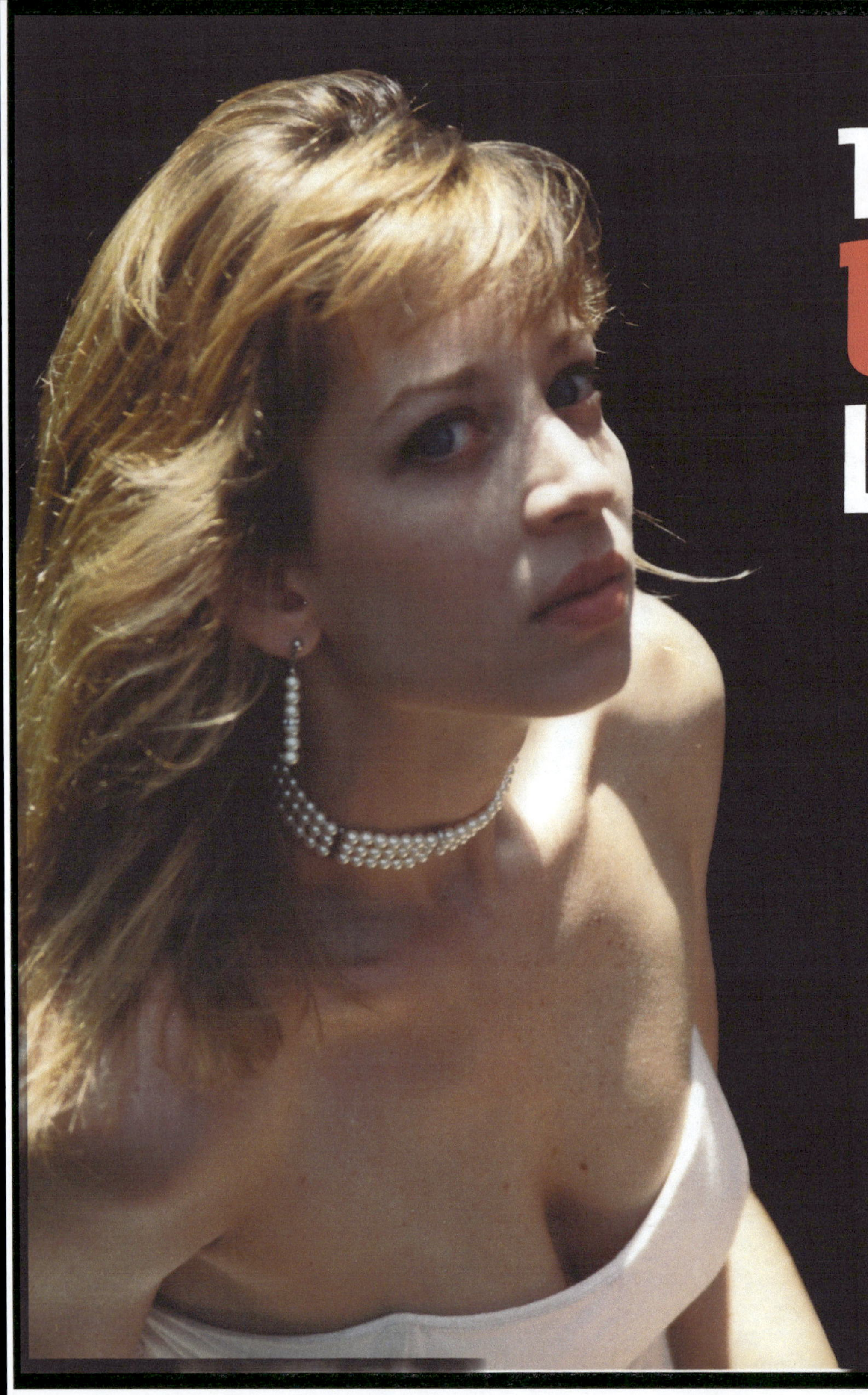

The First Steps In
EDUCATION
Last a Lifetime

SHARON
ESTHER
LAMPERT

SMARTGRADES
BRAIN POWER REVOLUTION

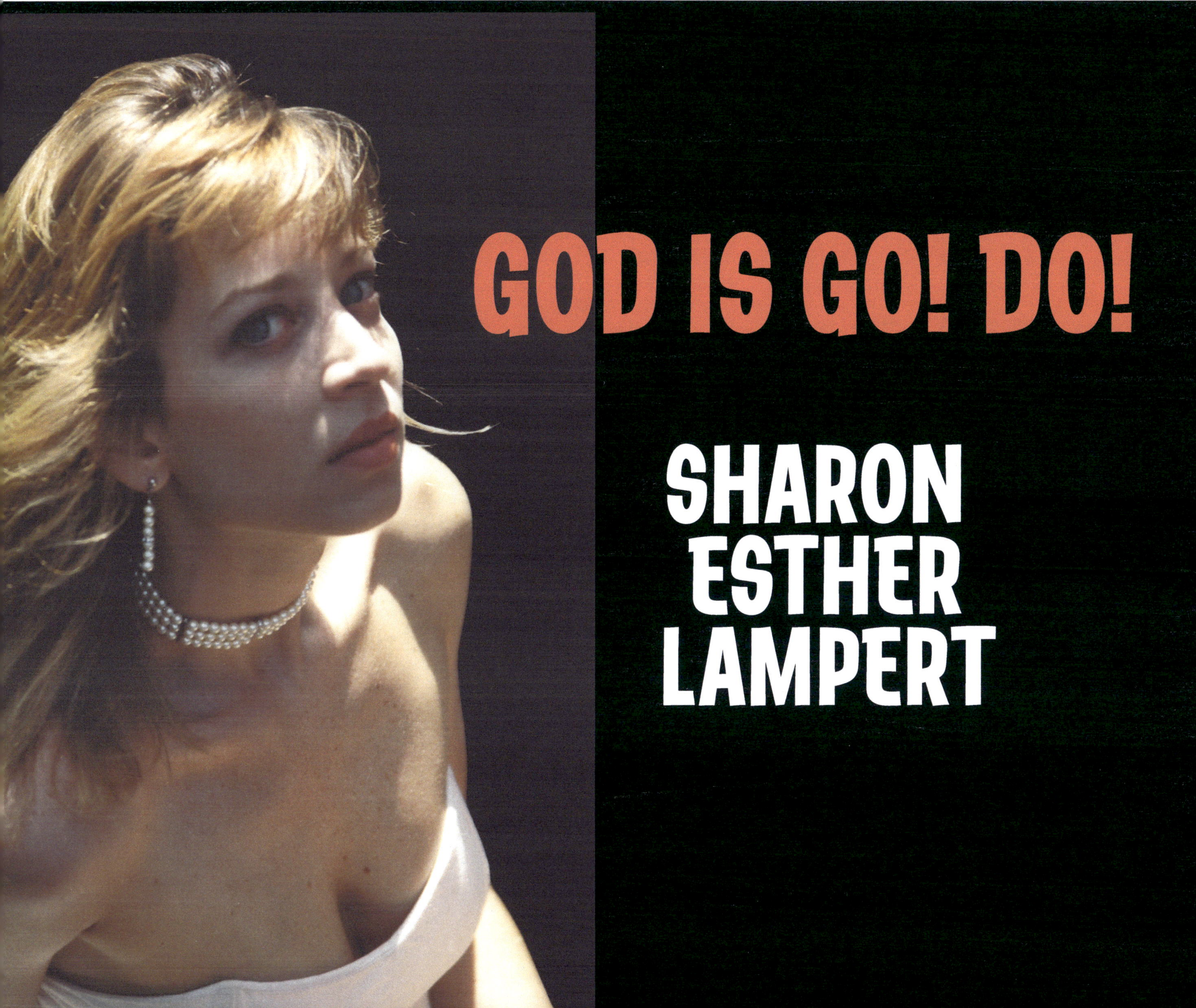
GOD IS GO! DO!
SHARON ESTHER LAMPERT

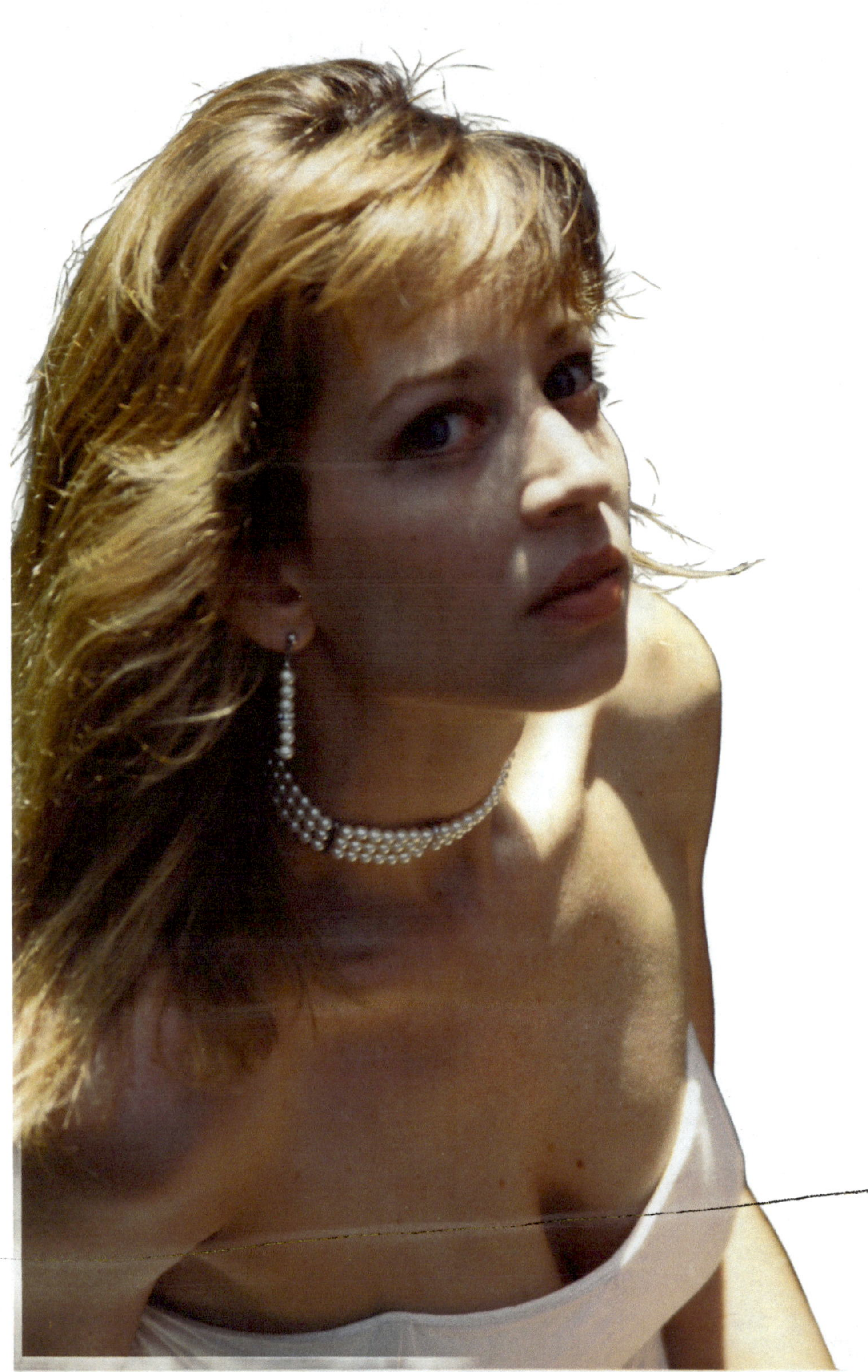


SHOPPING
IS BETTER
THAN SEX
LORD SEX and TAYLOR
BLOOMINGSEXDALES
BERGDORF GOODSEX
SEX FIFTH AVE
NORDSEX
MASEX
Sharon Esther Lampert

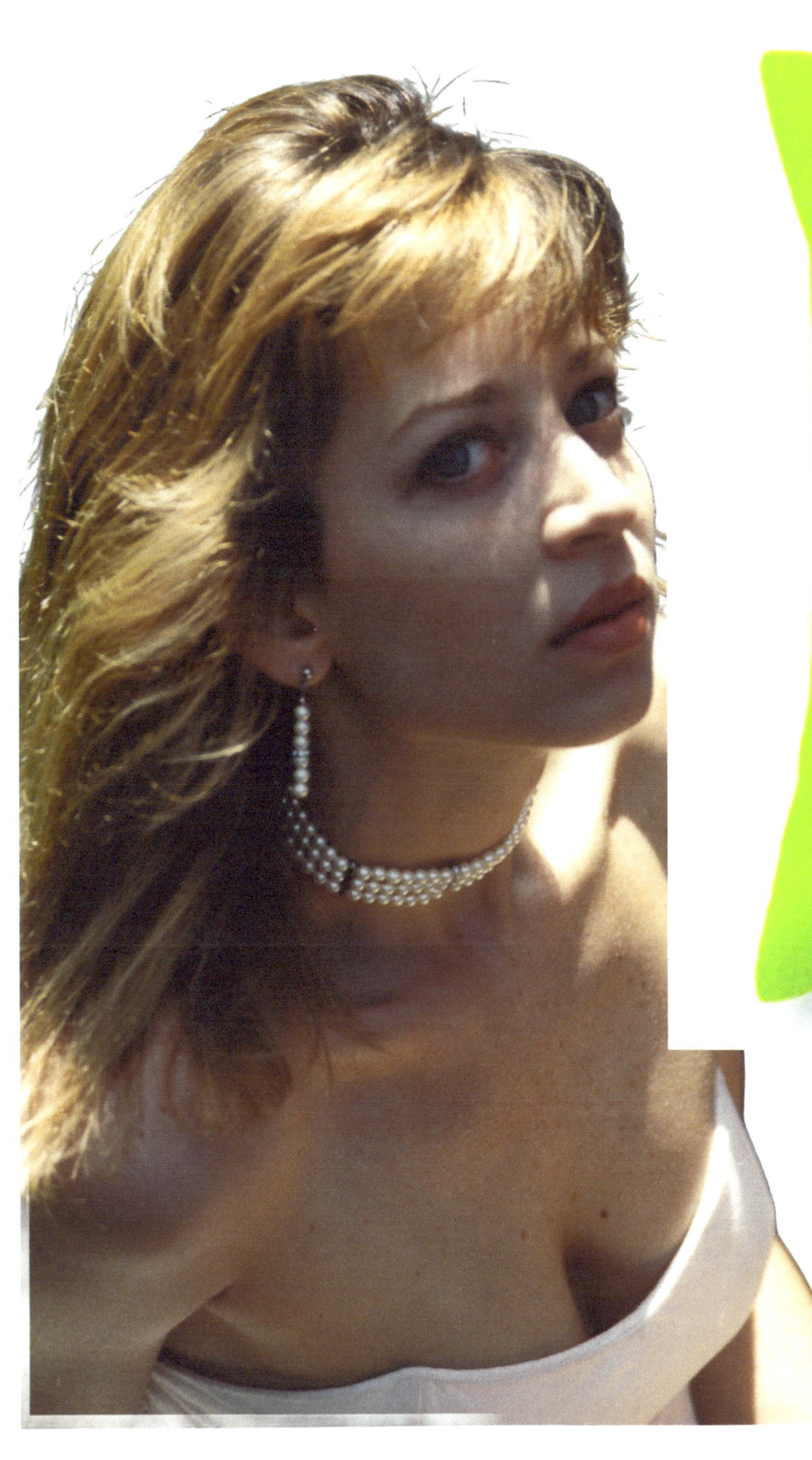


THERE IS
NO BOX
THAT CAN
HOLD ME
Sharon Esther Lampert
40
Fabulous
Colors

# What Happens When You Dress Up Albert Einstein As Marilyn Monroe?

## SHARON ESTHER LAMPERT

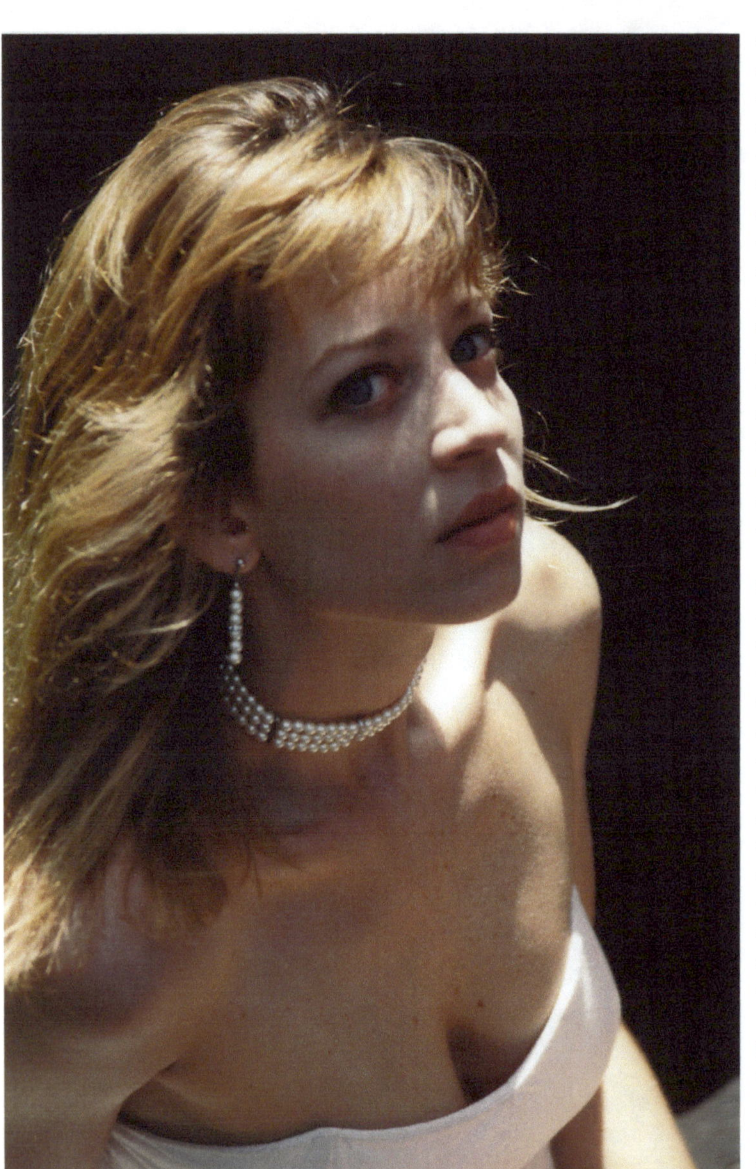

- Prodigy
- Poet
- Prophet
- Philosopher
- Peacemaker
- Paladin of Education
- **PHOTON SUPERHERO**
- Princess KADIMAH
- Princess & Pea
- Performer: Vocalist
- Player: Jock NYU Varsity B-Ball
- President
- Publisher
- Producer
- Psychobiologist:Rockefeller University
- Piano-Playing Cat
- Phoenix
- **PINUP**

**WEBSITES**
- SharonEstherLampert.com
- WorldFamousPoems.com
- PoetryJewels.com
- PhilosopherQueen.com
- GodIsGoDo.com
- Schmaltzy.com
- TrueLoveBurnsEternal.com
- SillyLittleBoys.com
- WinAtThin.com
- WritersRunTheWorld.com
- PalmBeachBookPublisher.com
- BooksArePowerful.com
- HappyGrandparenting.com
- WomenHaveAllThePower.com

**EDUCATION**
- Smartgrades.com
- PhotonSuperHero.com
- EveryDayAnEasyA.com
- BooksNotBombs.com

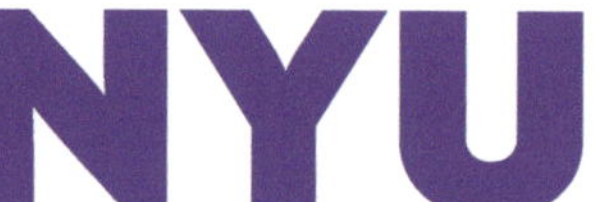

**AWARD for Multi-Interdisciplinary Studies**

Sharon Is Here There and Everywhere

# Honors & Awards

## NYU AWARD
Multi-Interdisciplinary Studies
NYU 3 Degrees: BA, MA, MA
NYU Varsity Basketball Team
NYU Weightlifting Contest

## NYC AWARD
100 Year Scholarship Award
Presented by NYC Mayor Koch

## NY EMPIRE STATE AWARD
Math and Science Scholarship

## JERUSALEM FELLOWSHIP
Aish Hatorah, Israel

## ROCKEFELLER UNIVERSITY
Science Paper Publication

## FIRST PRIZE
Upper East Side Resident
Newspaper Writing Contest

## FIRST PRIZE
THE WAVE (1893) Art Contest

## #1 POETRY WEBSITE
For Student Poetry Projects

## POETRY WORLD RECORD
120 Words of Rhyme from
One Family of Rhyme

# CONTRIBUTIONS TO CIVILIZATION
## Scientist, Artist, Educator, Peacemaker

## Published 80+ Books
### NYU: PERSTARE et PRAESTARE

### PRODIGY
10 Esoteric Laws of Genius and Creativity
Awesome Art of Alliteration Using One Letter of the Alphabet

### PROPHET
**GOD IS GO! DO!**
22 COMMANDMENTS: A UNIVERSAL MORAL COMPASS

### PHYSICIST
**LAWS OF INEXTRICABILITY - NEW SCIENTIFIC THEORY!**

### PSYCHOBIOLOGIST
**THE SPERM MANIFESTO: 10 RULES FOR THE ROAD -- NEW SCIENTIFIC THEORY!**

### PHILOSOPHER QUEEN
The Philosophy of Love: ME and WE
The Philosophy of Love: DOUBLE WHAMMY
Women Have All The Power But Have Never Have Learned How to Use It

### POET
### WORLD POETRY RECORD
**120 Words of Rhyme from One Family of Rhyme**
#1 Poetry Website for Student Projects
The Greatest Poems Ever Written on Extraordinary World Events
First Woman to Write a Book on 5000 Years of Jewish History in 6 Poetic Refrains

### PALADIN OF EDUCATION
SMARTGRADES BRAIN POWER REVOLUTION
8 Goalposts of Education
40 Universal Gold Standards of Education
SCHMALTZY: The FIrst Book of Color-Coded Words
Learn to Read Hebrew in One Hour

### PSYCHIATRIST
LOVE YOU MORE THAN YESTERDAY: 14 Relationship Strategies for Happily Ever After
Integration Therapy: Rebuild the Broken Wings of Students
3 Stages of Child Abuse
40 Rules of Manhood

### PEACEMAKER
WORLD PEACE EQUATION

### PINUP
SEXIEST GENIUS IN HUMAN HISTORY

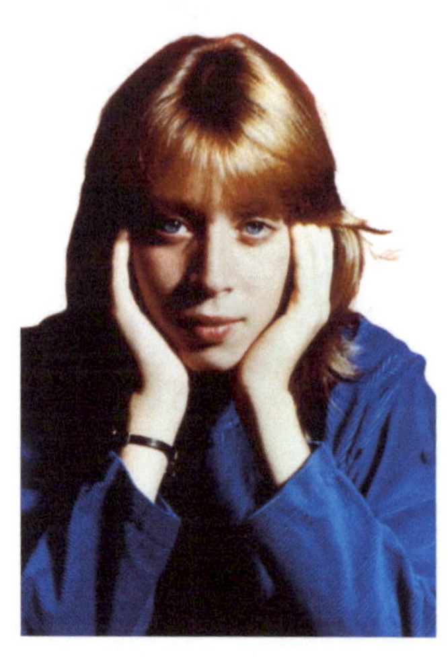

# GENIUS: THE GIFT OF DIVINE REVELATION

## MY BOOKS WRITE THEMSELVES

I Am Mortal
**MY BOOKS ARE IMMORTAL**
Please Handle My Books Gently
My Books Are My Remains

Part 1.  World Famous Quotes: 1997-2025
Part 2.  Format Book: January 2025
Part 3.  Publish: February 2025

Sharon Esther Lampert
SEE THE WORLD THROUGH THE EYES OF A CREATIVE GENIUS

Prodigy, Prophet, Philosopher, Poet, Peacemaker, Paladin of Education, Physicist, Princess

FANS@SharonEstherLampert.com

www.ingramcontent.com/pod-product-compliance
Lightning Source LLC
Chambersburg PA
CBHW041035120726

48006CB00005B/1193